DATA
PROCESSING
PROJECT
MANAGEMENT

DATA PROCESSING PROJECT MANAGEMENT

Second Edition

Thomas R. Gildersleeve

VNR VAN NOSTRAND REINHOLD COMPANY
———————————————— New York

Published by Van Nostrand Reinhold Company Inc.
135 West 50th Street
New York, New York 10020

Van Nostrand Reinhold Company Limited
Molly Millars Lane
Wokingham, Berkshire RG11 2PY, England

Van Nostrand Reinhold
480 Latrobe Street
Melbourne, Victoria 3000, Australia

Macmillan of Canada
Division of Gage Publishing Limited
164 Commander Boulevard
Agincourt, Ontario MIS 3C7, Canada

15 14 13 12 11 10 9 8 7 6 5 4 3 2 1

Library of Congress Cataloging in Publication Data

Gildersleeve, Thomas Robert.
  Data processing project management.

  Bibliography: p.
  Includes index.
  1. Electronic data processing departments—Management.
I. Title.
HF5548.2.G53   1984   658'.054   84-22082
ISBN 0-442-22851-1

To my father
Robert W. Gildersleeve

PREFACE

The second edition of this book represents a significant change from the first. But before discussing these changes, let's talk about what hasn't changed, namely, the book's structure. The first edition was the result of seven years of work. The first two years were spent practicing project management. Following these two years, a course on project management was developed, which was based on guidelines established by Robert E. Mager and Kenneth M. Beach, Jr. in their book, *Developing Vocational Instruction* (Fearon, 1967). The course was then honed through presentations to thousands of students, during which time, the book went through five rewrites before being submitted to the publisher. Given this tempering, if the book's structure had required change, it would have been a shock.

Since the publication of the first edition, much work has been done in the areas of project management and system development, and the book has been changed accordingly. For example, project management tools are described with increased precision. And system development related material has been replaced with references to other texts.

Another change in the second edition is in the tone of the book. The first edition described project management tools as if they should always be used full-force. In this edition, however, the point is emphasized that judgment must be exercised when applying these tools. Consequently, included with the description of tools is material for determining the extent to which tools should be employed.

Every effort has been made to make the information presented complete, clear, and concise. In particular

1. The section of the book on project organization now preceeds the section on project management prerequisites. It was felt that this reorganization would improve subject flow.
2. The titles of the chapters on manpower planning have been changed, although the subjects addressed remain the same. The change is a result of consciousness raising by the women's movement.
3. The chapter on computer time planning has been dropped, due to lack of interest in this subject.
4. Documentation (more properly a system development, rather than a project management topic), is now an appendix.
5. Originally the chapter on time reporting was included to recognize this activity as a factor in time estimating only. Since this recognition has been made in the literature, the material in this chapter has been incorporated into the section on time estimating.
6. The chapters on construction considerations, what managers can do to help project leaders, and most of the appendices, have been dropped, because the topics are now addressed in the literature.

Some of the material on project organization, listing tasks, and bubble charts is adapted from a course on PERT/CPM that I developed for Deltak, Inc.

CONTENTS

Date: May 16

Memo to: Marvin Melonhead
Department Head
Demitak Department

From: William Bluster
Manager
System Development

Copy to: Larry Leadpants
Analyst
System Development

Marv, I've just made our final review of your service request for a Corresponding System for your framistans. We're up to our ears here in System Development, but I can see that you've got a real problem, and we're here to help you out. I've appointed Larry Leadpants as project leader for the development of your system, and I've assigned project number 666 to the project. Our price for this project will be $72,000, and we don't see any reason why we can't meet your January 2 deadline. If all this is agreeable with you, just let us know, and we'll get Larry on the job.

Mary says she's looking forward to attending our reunion at Miasma U. with you and Helen. It sure will be good to see the old frat house boys after 15 years, won't it?

Date: May 23

Memo to: William Bluster
          Manager
          System Development

From: Marvin Melonhead
       Department Head
       Demitak Department

Bill, your figures look OK to me. If it will get us out of the mess we're in, $72,000 is cheap, especially when it's Chinese dollars. Tell Larry he's got my OK to speak to anyone on my staff to get the information he needs. I can hardly wait to start using the new system.

Date: June 24

Status Report

To: William Bluster
     Manager
     System Development

From: Larry Leadpants
       Analyst
       System Development

Project Number 666

A Correscoping System for the Demitak Department

I think we can say that the analysis on this project is just about over. Frankly,
I didn't get a lot of cooperation over at the Demitak Department. This guy
Anarchist is probably the most disorganized person I've ever run across.
Most of the time when I tried to see him he was busy with something else,
and when we did sit down to talk, he was always hopping up to handle the
crisis *de jour.*
   However, I've gotten a pretty good insight into the correscoping operation,
and frankly, it's just another file maintenance job. Everybody over there
seems to think they've got some unique problems, but you know how users
are.
   It looks like we're right on schedule. This week I'm going to start laying out
the design, and if everything goes according to plan, in a month I'll have the
system spec'ed out.

Date: July 21

Memo to: Larry Leadpants
               Analyst
               System Development

From: William Bluster
           Manager
           System Development

Frankly, Larry, I never got a chance to look at your status report before I
went on vacation at the end of June; and you know what a guy's desk looks
like when he gets back after two weeks away from the shop. Consequently, I
didn't read your report till yesterday.

   By now you must have the design of the Correscoping System just about
done. I'm sorry I didn't get into the act earlier. I sure would have liked to get
my hand in on the system layout. However, it's too late now. I've got all the
confidence in the world in you, Larry. I know you'll do a great job for
Demitak. Go to it, boy!

Date: July 29

Status Report

To: William Bluster
     Manager
     System Development

From: Larry Leadpants
       Analyst
       System Development

Project Number 666

A Correscoping System for the Demitak Department

I'm putting the finishing touches on the system design this week. We'll be
ready to put programmers on the job by Wednesday.

Date: August 4

Memo to: William Bluster
           Manager
           System Development

From: Larry Leadpants
        Analyst
        System Development

Bill—where are my programmers?

Date: August 8

Memo to: Larry Leadpants
Analyst
System Development

From: William Bluster
Manager
System Development

Chriminettles, Larry, give me a chance. You don't expect me to whomp up programmers out of thin air, do you? I'll get you some people as soon as I can.

Date: August 11

Memo to: Larry Leadpants
          Analyst
          System Programming

From: William Bluster
      Manager
      System Development

Beginning Monday, August 15, the following programmers will be assigned full-time to the development of the Correscoping System, project number 666.

1. Frederick Faithful
2. Elaine Eager

Date: August 12

Memo to: William Bluster
              Manager
              System Development

From: Larry Leadpants
          Analyst
          System Development

Holy cow Bill, what are you trying to do to me? You know that in the ten years Fred Faithful's been with us, he's never met a deadline. And Elaine Eager is right out of our entry level training program. At this rate, who can tell when we'll finish this project?

   Not so incidently, we need three programmers, not two. When can I expect the third member of my team?

Date: August 16

Memo to: Larry Leadpants
           Analyst
           System Programming

From: William Bluster
       Manager
       System Development

I'm really sorry about all this, Larry, but you know the problems we've got right now — we're putting in more new systems than ever before, maintenance work seems to be skyrocketing, and the brass is holding our budget to last year's level. Frankly, at this time, Faithful and Eager are the only people I can spare. I'll admit you've a few problems there, but it's nothing that a little supervision can't solve.

I'll try to get you a third person just as soon as I can. In the meantime Larry, perhaps you'd better roll up your sleeves and really dive into that programming work yourself.

I've got all the confidence in the world in you, Larry. I know you'll do a great job for Demitak. Go to it, boy!

Date: September 6

Memo to: Larry Leadpants
                Analyst
                System Development

From: William Bluster
            Manager
            System Development

Beginning Wednesday, September 7, Suki So-so will be assigned full-time to the development of the Correscoping System, project number 666.

Date: September 12

Memo to: Larry Leadpants
              Analyst
              System Development

From: William Bluster
          Manager
          System Development

Larry, what's going on? For the past month you've been bugging me for another programmer. So even though it's hurting, I took So-so off the Pulsitran System and gave him to you. Today I walked past Suki's desk, and he's working crossword puzzles!!! Larry, what's going on?

Date: September 12

Memo to: William Bluster
　　　　　Manager
　　　　　System Development

From: Larry Leadpants
　　　　Analyst
　　　　System Development

Sorry about this So-so business, Bill. Frankly, since you gave me Suki last Wednesday, I've been

1. Keeping on Faithful's tail so he stays out of the coffeeshop and finishes up the Edit Program he was supposed to have coded two weeks ago.
2. Working with Elaine Eager a couple of hours every day to teach her enough programming so she can get her work done.
3. Trying to get enough done on the Update Program (for which I assumed responsibility in the absence of any other programmer on the team) so it wouldn't slip so far behind that it would hold up Fred and Elaine when they need it.

I just haven't had enough time leftover to brief Suki on the job I have for him. However, even though it will hurt, I'll ignore these other responsibilities for a few days and get Suki into the Phase Three Program, which as you know, is the heart of the Correscoping System.

Bill, I did want to say that I appreciate your assigning Suki to the team. He's just the person to handle the Phase Three Program, and it's a weight off my mind.

Date: September 23

Status Report

To: William Bluster
      Manager
      System Programming

From: Larry Leadpants
        Analyst
        System Development

Project Number 666

A Corresponding System for the Demitak Department

Well, things are beginning to look up. I still have to dog Faithful to keep him
on the job, but Elaine Eager is beginning to shape up into a real programmer.
I'm beginning to rely on her more and more heavily. And Suki So-so has sure
torn into the Phase Three Program. He's already taken it far beyond the point
to which I had worked it out, and although I sometimes worry about the fact
that he carries so much of what he's doing around in his head, he certainly is
turning out the code.

Date: September 26

Memo to: Larry Leadpants
          Analyst
          System Development

From: William Bluster
       Manager
       System Development

Larry, I really hate to do this to you, but over the weekend the Pulistran
System blew up higher than a kite. The boys seem to think the trouble is in
Suki's program, and you know the kind of documentation he leaves behind.
I'm afraid I'm going to have to pull Suki off the Correscoping System till we
get the Pulsitran System straightened out. It may be a week or two. Larry,
I'm sorry.

Date: September 26

Memo to: William Bluster
          Manager
          System Development

From: Larry Leadpants
       Analyst
       System Development

. . . help!

Date: October 7

Status Report

To: William Bluster
Manager
System Development

From: Larry Leadpants
Analyst
System Development

Project Number 666

A Corresponding System for the Demitak Department

Here's the situation:

1. Faithful is performing in his usual manner, which means that he keeps falling behind. At least the work he does turn out is pretty reliable, and I'm keeping after him.
2. Elaine Eager is really beginning to blossom. As soon as she finishes the scut work she's been doing, I'm going to assign her to the Phase Two Program.
3. Suki finally returned to us Wednesday, and is now back hard at work. Nevertheless, we've lost about another two weeks on Phase Three.

In general, we're somewhat behind, and we're just going to have to start putting in some overtime.

Date: October 31

Memo to: William Bluster
                 Manager
                 System Development

From: Marvin Melonhead
            Department Head
            Demitak Department

Bill, Archie Anarchist has just come up with a brilliant idea for improving our framistan operation. He hasn't got all the details worked out yet, but before you get the Correscoping System cast in concrete, why don't you have Larry Leadpants get together with Archie to see what, if any, affect his ideas will have on the system?

   Bill, I can't tell you how much we're looking forward to the beginning of the year when we'll start using your new data processing system to bail us out of the paperwork mess we're in now. I only wish I could have been closer to the whole thing. However, I've got all the confidence in the world in you, Bill. I know you'll do a great job for Demitak. Keep up the good work!

Date: November 3

Memo to: Marvin Melonhead
          Department Head
          Demitak Department

From: William Bluster
       Manager
       System Development

Copy to: Larry Leadpants
          Analyst
          System Development

Marv, it's good to hear those kind words. Of course, we'll see what we can do to help out Archie Anarchist. After all, if we don't provide service, what are we for?

   By copy of this memo I'm asking Larry to get together with Archie and find out what Archie's thoughts are on the framistan operation.

Date: November 8

Memo to: William Bluster
          Manager
          System Development

From: Larry Leadpants
       Analyst
       System Development

Bill, I finally got together with Archie Anarchist, and does he have ideas! The
way he's talking now, a good bit of the work we've done on the Update
Program, and almost everything we've put into Phase Three is down the
drain.

   We're not going to meet that January 2 date, Bill. I recommend that we tell
Demitak now, so they can adjust to the change.

Date: November 9

Memo to: Larry Leadpants
           Analyst
           System Development

From: William Bluster
      Manager
      System Development

Larry, I'm trying to get my five year plan past Ben Bigdome's desk. All I need now is a big slip on a major project.

   For Pete's sale, get in there with Archie Anarchist and get these changes nailed down, and then pour on the coal! In the meantime, I'll see if I can get you another pair of hands.

Date: November 25

Status Report

To: William Bluster
     Manager
     System Development

From: Larry Leadpants
       Analyst
       System Development

Project Number 666

A Corresponding System for the Demitak Department

In the past two weeks the functional specifications for this system have
undergone major revision three separate times. However, I think we've finally
got them the way Anarchist wants them, and we're now back trying to
recover lost time. I'm afraid overtime has become a way of life on the
project.

   I want to thank you for the extra person you assigned to the project.

   Elaine Eager has finished Phase Two, and I've got her helping Suki with
Phase Three. That girl is really a comer, but of late her work has been getting
a little ragged. She tells me her boyfriend has broken up with her, and she
has headaches almost everyday. She says if overtime doesn't stop soon,
she's going to quit.

Date: December 5

Memo to: William Bluster
          Manager
          System Development

From: Larry Leadpants
       Analyst
       System Development

Bill, we need a replacement for Elaine Eager.

Date: December 23

Status Report

To: William Bluster
     Manager
     System Development

From: Larry Leadpants
       Analyst
       System Development

Project Number 666

A Correscoping System for the Demitak Department

We're putting the final touches on the programs and are ready to go into link
test. Unfortunately, I haven't yet had time to prepare the link test data.

Any day now we should probably tell Demitak we aren't going to make the
January 2 date.

It also occurred to me that, to put the system on the air, we're going to
have to convert all those ledger cards over there in Demitak to disk. That's
no mean task, and we better institute a crash effort to get the job done. I
figure that two more people in addition to the project team ought to be able
to do the job in three weeks.

Date: December 28

Memo to: All Vice Presidents, Department Heads, and Managers

From: Peter Pompous
        President
        Quasi Corporation

It is with regret that we announce that Marvin Melonhead, our good friend
and former Head of the Demitak Department, has resigned his position to
take on new and challenging work. However, Quasi Corp. has never been
unmindful of its larger responsibilities to the society that nourishes us all, and
we are happy to know that, in some small measure, we have prepared Marv
for his new venture. Therefore, it is with mixed feelings of regret and pride
that we wish Marv Godspeed and good luck in his new position as Head
Janitor at Miasma University.

   We are fortunate in being able to replace Marv with a man who brings
many years of experience to his job. It is my pleasure to announce the
appointment of Warren Windy to the position of Department Head, Demitak
Department. I know you will all show Warren the courtesy for which Quasi is
famous and give him your utmost in cooperation.

   Warren comes to us from a series of responsible positions at Miasma
University, the last of which was Head Janitor.

Date: January 5

Memo to: William Bluster
Manager
System Development

From: Warren Windy
Department Head
Demitak Department

It has recently been brought to my attention that there is, in development in your shop, a "Correscoping System" for our framistan operation. Since I'm rather new on the job, I'm wondering if we can't get together someday soon, perhaps over lunch, to discuss this system. I've reviewed the correspondence, but I'm not sure I quite grasp the system's purpose.

Date: January 10

Memo to: Larry Leadpants
            Analyst
            System Development

From: William Bluster
         Manager
         System Development

Larry, I just got back from a long and rather uncomfortable luncheon with
Warren Windy. He doesn't seem to be at all convinced that our Correscoping
System is what his framistan operation needs. However, I did manage to get
him to agree that the major investment in system development has already
been made, and that it would be unjustified to not go ahead and finish the
work we've started. Consequently, it looks like we've got the green light.
   You're doing a great job, Larry. Keep up the good work!

Date: February 15

Memo to: Archibald Anarchist
          Assistant Department Head
          Demitak Department

From: Larry Leadpants
       Analyst
       System Development

As you know, Archie, we completed the conversion of your master file last Wednesday.

Last night our system processed the test data we developed for it without a hitch.

Consequently, we'd like to cut over to the new system on Monday and have you take the responsibility for the operation of the system.

Date: February 17

Memo to: William Bluster
                  Manager
                  System Development

From: Archibald Anarchist
            Assistant Department Head
            Demitak Department

Copies to: Warren Windy
                   Department Head
                   Demitak Department

                   Benjamin Bigdome
                   Director
                   Data Processing

With reference to Mr. Larry Leadpants' memo of February 15, a copy of which is attached:
    The chaos in our operation that has resulted from the conversion of our historical data to disk leaves us with no alternative but to acquiesce in the February 20 cutover to the new Correscoping System. However:

1. A preliminary review of the system test results supplied to us by Mr. Leadpants indicates that the designers of the new system suffered under some gross misconceptions as to procedures in the framistan operation. Documentation to support this contention is attached. Review of system results by the Demitak Department will continue, and periodically you will be informed of all other deficiencies unearthed.
2. The Demitak Department is totally without the facilities to operate the new Correscoping System. No written procedures for the new system exist, and none of our personnel have received any briefing, let alone training, on how to carry out their new responsibilities. As a consequence, until procedures are documented and the personnel are trained, our staff will follow the old procedures, and your department will have to effect the required adjustments to make our operation compatible with the new system.

    Until these operational, documentation, and educational difficulties are cleared up, responsibility for the Correscoping System must remain with the Data Processing Department.

Date: April 13

Report

Post-Installation Review

To: William Bluster
     Manager
     System Development

From: System Review Committee

       Project Number 666

A Correscoping System for the Demitak Department

This project was officially closed on March 30. On that date, by direction of Mr. Peter Pompous, President of Quasi Corporation, the Demitak Department accepted responsibility for the Correscoping System. Mr. Pompous accounted for his action by saying that he felt the remaining problems with this system would be cleared up more quickly if responsibility for the system was in the hands of the operating department originally requesting the system. In accepting the system, Mr. Warren Windy, Operating Head of the Demitak Department, said that he did so under protest, that he didn't see why he should have to clean up someone else's mess, and he swore he would never let the Data Processing Department do anything for him again. He said he'd rather hire his own programmers, if that's what it took.

Thus, the Correscoping System was officially delivered exactly three months after its committed delivery date, although troubles with the system remain, and it is expected that for a period of at least six months, the maintenance load for this system will be high.

Development cost for this project overran the Data Processing Department's original quotation by 95%.

A comparison of the operation of this system with the original objectives set forth for it reveals the following:

1. The normal file maintenance operation of the system is performing similarly to the previous manual system. Mistakes still occur, but since March 7, when 27,534 master records were misplaced, no loss of information has occurred. It's expected that these difficulties are temporary and that normal maintenance operations will clear them up. The Demitak Department now estimates that in the next two years, it will have to increase its clerical work force by only 50% rather than by 100%. The department is dissatisfied with this reduction, but it's impossible to tell whether the system has met its objective in this area, since the objective was never quantified.

2. The lag between closing and production of summary reports has been reduced to an average of 22 working days. Most of the delay in this area can be attributed to the need for reruns, because of inconsistencies found in the reports produced. It is expected that when the system is shaken down, the goal of a maximum lag of 10 working days will be realized.

3. As near as can be determined by the committee, the system's ability to produce special reports appears to have met the objective originally set for it. The reason it is necessary to be vague in this area is because this feature has never been subjected to a real life test. Demitak personnel are so disenchanted by their initial experiences with the system that they now refuse to use it. Management continues to run the framistan operation the way they always have.

4. The system has managed to reduce, but not yet eliminate, the crisis associated with production of government reports. As bugs in the system are corrected, continued performance improvement in this area is anticipated.

In summary, it must be said that, despite its difficulties, the Correscoping System is not a bad system. As soon as its current error rate is reduced through continued maintenance, it will undoubtedly be of some benefit to the Demitak Department. However, it was not designed to fit in smoothly with the framistan operation; consequently, it is somewhat awkward to use. This ackwardness, coupled with the series of disasters to which the Demitak personnel were subjected during development and installation of the system has, in their eyes, largely eliminated any benefits to be gained from the system. The system has not made any friends for the Data Processing Department; Data Processing has certainly gained some short-term, if not long-term, enemies. Moreover, if Demitak had it to do over again, it would probably stick with its old system.

In addition to the difficulties in the Demitak Department, the Correscoping System has also caused corporate-wide operating problems. The auditors say that the system has been put together in such a way that it's practically impossible to establish an audit trail. Also, the figures produced by the system are not compatible with corporate general ledger accounting practices, so at present, considerable manual manipulation of these figures must be done before they can be passed on to the accountants. In Data Processing's defense, it must be said that the original Request for Services by Demitak specifically eliminated such corporate considerations from the scope of the system. But as the new Demitak Department Head points out, only an incompetent department head could have taken it on himself to establish such limitations. Moreover, besides the general difficulties with which the Data Processing Department finds itself, it's faulted for not being smart enough to ignore the limitations of scope mistakenly imposed on the system by the former Demitak Department Head.

Date: April 16

Memo to: Benjamin Bigdome
           Director
           Data Processing

From: William Bluster
        Manager
        System Development

I'm enclosing a copy of the Post-Installation Review Report prepared by the
System Review Committee on Project 666, The Correscoping System.
    As you can see, we didn't cover ourselves with glory.
    I don't think it's too hard to pinpoint our difficulty. Frankly, I never did
have much confidence in Larry Leadpants, but at the time of Demitak's
request, he was the only person available to assign to the job.

Date: May 16

Memo to: Larry Leadpants
          Analyst
          System Development

From: Personnel Department

This is to confirm that your exit interview will be conducted at 11 A.M. on
Friday, May 18, at these offices. At that time, your termination check will be
available for you to pick up.

The question is: Where did Larry Leadpants go wrong?

Before reading on, formulate your answer to this question. Then continue reading to get our opinion.

Some people say Larry's mistake was to work for the wrong company. Bluster has the earmarks of a scoundrel. And Demitak's role in the development of the Correscoping System was confused. We admit that, in fabricating this data processing tragedy, we overstated the situation. But exaggerated though it may be, we defy anybody to examine the regrettable and unsavory traits exhibited by the personae who collectively contributed to Larry's downfall and deny that such traits exist in the ranks of system development management and user personnel.

But everyone must be prepared for the likelihood that the people with whom he deals are imperfect. We each have a responsibility to protect ourselves from the failures of those around us. Consequently, no one can lay the blame for a personal catastrophe at another person's door. The object isn't that everyone must look out for himself, but rather that, if we each protect ourselves against the failures of others, we protect ourselves collectively from common disaster. We fault Larry for the following:

1. He accepted a fixed *deadline* and *budget* before he knew what he had to deliver. Consequently, he missed his deadline by three months and overran his budget by 95%.
2. The design of the system was never reviewed by the people in the corporation who are concerned with the design of all data processing systems regardless of user. Consequently, these people couldn't live with the new system (the auditors couldn't establish an audit trail).
3. He didn't get prior agreement with the user as to what constituted acceptable system operation. Consequently, when he decided the system was acceptable and tried to turn it over to the user, the user wouldn't accept it.
4. He didn't plan the resources needed to reach his goal. Consequently:
   a. He was surprised by the need to perform tasks (*file conversion*, *user manual* writing, *user training*), for which he had made no provisions.
   b. He found himself trying to accomplish tasks for which he had inadequate resources (not enough personnel and insufficiently skilled personnel). And from time to time, resources were yanked out from under him with no relaxation on his commitments.
   c. He found himself personnally committed to detailed tasks (coding a major program), which resulted in his inability to handle his project leader responsibilities.
   d. He subjected his staff to unreasonable demands (overtime as a way of life).

You may think Larry's experience was a total disaster. To the contrary, Larry stumbled into only a few of the pitfalls waiting for the unwary project leader.

The purpose of this book is to acquaint you with the mistakes a project leader can make and show you how to avoid them. Thus armed, you can carry out your project leader responsibilities without experiencing disaster.

The negative phrasing of the book's purpose is intentional. The techniques recommended in this book won't make project management a breeze, and use of the techniques isn't easy. Undertaking a project involves trying something that, to some extent, has never been done before. You can expect such a job to be fraught with frustration, aggravation, problems, and setbacks. If you don't want to subject yourself to this kind of heat, take President Truman's advice and stay out of the kitchen. However, if you're willing to wrestle with the problems of project management, there's no reason why your efforts should result in catastrophe. This book shows you how to be a project leader, how to deliver on your commitments, and how to keep your reputation intact.

PROJECT ORGANIZATION

The type of work known as a *project* has existed throughout history. For example, building a pyramid was a project. However, it wasn't until after World War II that the term project took on organizational meaning. Prior to this, there were only two formally recognized ways of organizing work. One way was through *decentralization*, typified and first put into practice by Sloan's organization of numerous automobile operations, which later became General Motors.

2.1 FUNCTIONAL ORGANIZATION

The other formal way of organizing work was by *function*. This technique was first described by the Frenchman Henri Fayol. According to Fayol, work should be organized on the basis of the functions it carries out. Thus, the typical manufacturing company is organized into an engineering department, a production facility, a marketing operation, and so on. While decentralization was a technique for subdividing a giant company into manageable parts, each decentralized unit was organized functionally.

The object of *functional organization* is to develop and maintain expertise. It encourages people to specialize and become experts in particular functions. Functional organization works well for a unit engaged in a single, integrated activity. Thus, Fayol ran a coal company, which influenced his thinking with

40

respect to organization principles. However, when a company's activities diversify, the weaknesses in functional organization appear.

2.2 PROJECT ORGANIZATION

A work unit can have the responsibility for concurrently attaining several *goals*. For example, a *system development department* may be required to develop an order entry system, an accounts receivable system, and a personnel system—all at the same time.

These concurrently running efforts require various skills to reach the desired goals. Consequently, in a functional organization, the unit manager must coordinate each of these efforts or coordination becomes fragmented among the functional supervisors. The first alternative is usually impossible, and the second isn't desirable, since fragmented coordination typically is lack of coordination.

The manager solves this problem by delegating his responsibilities for a particular effort, or project, to a project leader. In this way, a *project organization* is created.

Project organization institutionalizes the conflicts that arise between attaining the project goal and other activities in which the unit is engaged. Thus, conflicts are brought into the open, and the manager can resolve them in the light of the overall situation.

Project organization can be implemented in several ways:

1. Personnel with the required skills are selected for assignment to a *project team*. For the life of the project, members of the team take direction from the project leader.
2. Each functional supervisor coordinates those project activities for which he has functional responsibility. The project leader monitors the activities of the functional groups to see that they mesh in such a way that the project goal is achieved.
3. Various combinations of the above two approaches can be adopted.

The first type of organization implementation is typical of projects involving small numbers of people, while the second is typical of projects involving large numbers of people. The rest of this book deals with the first type of project organization.

2.3 TYPES OF WORK

The concept of project management recognizes that there's more than one type of work. One factor that must be distinguished is whether the work is *goods* or *goal* oriented (where the concept of services is included in the concept of goods).

This does not imply, however, that goods oriented work doesn't have goals. Instead, the term goal is used in a restricted sense. Perhaps the best way to explain our use of the word goal is to give some examples.

2.3.1 Goods Oriented

Manufacturing—such as producing cars, detergents, and clothing—is goods oriented work. Other goods oriented work includes running a cinema, a grocery store, a travel service, and other kinds of retailing. These activities have goals, namely, certain revenue or profit levels. But having reached a goal, these activities don't cease. Instead, the goals are either rejuvenated or replaced. When a goods oriented activity ceases, it's the result of some external event, such as diminution of demand, or death or retirement of the retailer.

2.3.2 Goal Oriented

In contrast, work with a limited lifespan is referred to as goal oriented work. For example, climbing Mt. Everest is a well-defined goal, which includes getting back down as well as scaling the peak. Once the goal is reached, the activity oriented toward the goal ceases.

While it's possible to identify goal oriented work, there's some confusion in this area. Thus, it's necessary to keep an eye on distinctions to avoid being overwhelmed by complications.

For example, at the end of a goal oriented activity, there's sometimes *follow-on work*. For the person who scales Mt. Everest, such follow-on work consists of writing books and articles, and giving talks on the lecture circuit. Similarly, the development and installation of a data processing system has follow-on work, namely, the enhancement of the system. This follow-on work, however, must not be confused with the original goal oriented work.

Also, while manufacturing and retailing are goods oriented work, they sometimes incorporate goal oriented work within their framework. For instance, manufacturers, to ensure or augment their profitability, bring new products to the market. Similarly, retailers open new outlets and departments. Each such practice is goal oriented and can be managed as a project.

Finally, we must distinguish between goal oriented activities and the units that carry them out. The attainment of the goal, and consequently, the demise of the activity, doesn't necessarily imply the end of the unit carrying out the activity. When Mt. Everest is scaled, the expedition organized for the ascent is disbanded. Dispersal of the unit at the end of a project is often the case. It's typical of goal oriented activities carried out by goods oriented companies.

However, this is not always the case. For example the March of Dimes had the goal of wiping out polio. When it achieved its goal, it survived by finding a

ORIENTATION	TECHNIQUES	
	KNOWN	UNKNOWN
Goods-Oriented	Manufacturing, Retailing, etc.	Nonexistent
Goal-Oriented	Project	Research

Figure 2-1. Types of work.

substitute goal—the elimination of birth defects. By adopting this substitute goal, the March of Dimes tried to guarantee its continued existence by choosing a goal that can probably never be completely achieved.

2.3.3 Research

We've thus far identified several examples of goal oriented activities—scaling Mt. Everest, putting a new product on the market, opening a new store, and wiping out polio. However, not all of these activities are projects. To be a project, the goal oriented activity must use known techniques to reach its goal. Thus, if a project fails to reach its goal, it's not for lack of knowledge on how to reach the goal. Goal oriented activities that fail to meet this criterion are *research*. Thus, wiping out polio, although a goal oriented activity, wasn't a project because the techniques for reaching the goal had not been known; a part of attaining the goal was determination of these techniques. Thus, cancer research today is a goal oriented activity but isn't a project.

Although we hear reference to research projects, in this book, research isn't a project. While specific research activities, such as determination of whether a given drug produces the desired effects, are projects, searching for techniques isn't a project. These ideas are summarized in Figure 2–1.

2.4 SUMMARY

1. A project is an organized effort to reach a predefined goal. The goal is unique, and when reached, the project is over. The landing of a person on the moon, the climbing of a challenging mountain peak, the turnover of a new model car to production, and the implementation of a new demand deposit data processing system are all projects. Orientation of the project toward a unique, terminal goal contrasts with activities such as mass production of cars and updating passbooks, which are activities done over and over again.
2. Projects are also distinguished from research. Projects and research share the characteristic of goal uniqueness, but they differ in that a project goal is

predefined, while a research goal is vague. Research is concerned with developing technologies to reach predefined goals.

3. The essence of project management is that one person, the project leader, is given responsibility for attainment of the project goal—on schedule, within budget, and according to specifications.

4. Attainment of a project goal requires the use of several specialties. This requirement is satisfied by assembling a project team, made up of people possessing required specialities, that reports to the project leader.

5. A project competes, with the other activities of the unit of which it's a part, for the unit's scarce resources. The function of project organization is to provide the unit manager with an informed picture of the project's needs, so they can be properly weighted in the manager's resource allocation decisions.

Thus, the reason your manager makes you a project leader is because he wants a predefined goal to be achieved on schedule, within budget, and according to specifications. He gives this assignment to you and puts certain resources under your control. He wants you to use these resources efficiently and effectively. He wants you to work within his organization to acquire any other resources you need to attain the project goal. And if you run into difficulties beyond your control, he expects to be informed, so he can take your needs into consideration in his resource allocation decisions.

PROJECT PREREQUISITES

The three prerequisites to successful project management are as follows:

1. The project leader must know who his *user* is.
2. The system development department must support a *phased approach to system development*.
3. The project leader must know when the project ends. The way to mark the end of system development is to have the system pass an *acceptance test*.

3.1 THE USER

The system development department is a service organization whose operations produce no revenue. Its contribution is to help other departments cut costs and increase revenue through use of systems developed for this purpose. The success of the system development department depends on its ability to satisfy system users. Your success as a project leader depends on an identification of the user of the system your project is going to develop.

3.1.1 The Need For User Identification

User identification isn't your responsibility. It's a decision that should be made for you. It shouldn't be up to a project leader to decide how his organization's data processing resources are used. When developing a data processing system, you'll be working with the people who will use the system. In a general sense, all of these people are users. However, in a project management sense, there's just one user. He's the person who ultimately decides what the system will and won't do. In this book, we use the singular form of the word "user" to refer to the concept of user in the project management sense. When we use the word "user" in the general sense, however, we use the plural, "users" or we use the word "user" in combination with other words (e.g. user personnel).

The user delegates most of his decisions to the people who'll work most closely with the system. Occasionally, one of these people will say that the system should do one thing, while another maintains that some other, incompatible thing should be done. When a mutually agreeable compromise cannot be reached, it's not up to you to resolve such disagreements; this is the user's job. Thus, the user speaks with one voice and must have the authority to do so.

3.1.2 Documenting the User Identification

Your user identification must be documented. How this is done depends on the situation.

There may be a form, which is completed at the beginning of a project, that identifies the user. If so, be sure you have a copy of the form. If a copy isn't routed to you, don't be obnoxious about getting a copy. Just casually mention to your manager at an appropriate moment that you'd find it convenient, for completeness of your project records, to have a copy. Your manager will be so delighted to find that you're keeping a complete set of project records that he'll be happy to give you a copy.

If there is no form or other document identifying your user, but your user has been identified to you verbally, document this information. Again, don't be obnoxious. If you periodically write a *status report* on your project, include the user identification in your first status report. If you are not producing status reports, write a memo describing the initiation of the project and include the user identification in this memo.

If you're unclear as to who your user is, discuss it with your manager. A user identification normally develops out of such a discussion. If it doesn't, you must decide who your user is. In either case, document the identification with the appropriate technique as described in the preceding paragraph.

3.1.3 Examples

Let's apply the above principles to some example situations.

Your project is to develop a production control system. Who's your user?

Who the user is, is a good question. If you work with the manufacturing department to develop a system that can be used to control its operations, you leave yourself open to the charge that you ignored management's needs for information. On the other hand, if you build a management information system, you can be accused of making a career out of a request for a simple manufacturing control system. Thus, it is wise to get some clarification.

Your company has 67 branch offices. Your project is to develop a common order entry system for all 67 branches. Who's your user?

Again, the question remains open. However, one thing which is certain is that, although you'll spend a good bit of time working with the branch offices, they don't collectively make up your user. The user is more likely to be the head of the department in the home office to whom the branches report.

You work for a computer manufacturer. Your project is to build a software package for a computer system manufactured by your company. Who's your user—your company or your company's customers?

Your company's customers are analogous to the branch offices in the above example. But your company isn't your user either. The user is a person, not an organization. You must determine who's to speak for your company on the project. Typically, there's a product manager in charge of the computer system for which you're to build the software package. He's a likely candidate for the role of the user.

You work for a company organized into three departments. Your project is to develop a system to be used by all three departments. Who's your user?

Your user is the person to whom all the departments report, namely the company president or someone on his staff to whom he delegates his user responsibility.

3.2 THE PHASED APPROACH TO SYSTEM DEVELOPMENT

One of Larry Leadpants' problems was that he committed himself to a budget before he knew what it was he had to deliver. A way to avoid this problem is to refuse to develop a cost estimate until you know what you have to do.

But let's look at the situation through your user's eyes. He's saying, "You, Mr. System Development Person, want to spend money ostensibly on my behalf. You want to come into my department, disrupt my operations, and tie up my personnel in interviews, and you want me to agree to all this without knowing what it's going to cost. Without this information, how can I tell whether any of this is worthwhile?" The user has a point.

This is a dilemma. X (the user) is saying to Y (the system development department), "I can't give you *A* (a system definition) until you give me *B* (the system development costs)." And *Y* is saying to *X*, "I can't give you *B* until you give me *A*." The solution to this problem is a phased approach in which reciprocal commitments are made in a graduated way that allows each side to provide useful information to the other without prematurely committing either party.

3.2.1 The Phased Approach

The phased approach to system development in its undiluted form is as follows:

1. An initial *cost benefit analysis* is made.
2. If the cost benefit analysis indicates that the system should be developed, the first phase in system development is undertaken.
3. At the end of the first phase, costs and benefits can be estimated with greater accuracy. These more accurate costs and benefits are used to make a second cost benefit analysis.
4. If this cost benefit analysis indicates that development should continue, the next phase is undertaken.
5. At the end of this phase, cost and benefit estimates are again refined, and another cost benefit analysis is made.

Steps 4 and 5 are repeated until either

1. The cost benefit analysis indicates that further work should be abandoned.
2. The last development phase is completed, resulting in an operating system.

For a description of how to do a cost benefit analysis, see the chapter on "Cost Benefit Analysis" in *Successful Data Processing System Analysis*.

The idea behind the phased approach to system development is that, with each succeeding phase, the system definition is more detailed. Consequently, cost and benefit estimates become progressively more reliable, and the feasibility decisions based on these estimates become increasingly realistic.

The division of system development into phases is arbitrary. However, the larger the development effort, the more phases into which it's divided. Some commonly used phases are as follows:

1. Initiation—In the initiation phase, the user and the system development department invest the minimum amount of resources to provide the user with enough information to decide whether he wants to pursue development of the system.
2. Functional Specification—The user and the system development department agree on system functions.

3. Design—The way the system is to be constructed to perform its functions is documented, and every part of the company with an interest in the design of its data processing system agree on the acceptability of the contents of this documentation.
4. Construction—The system development department builds and installs the system.

For more on development phases, see the "Introduction" to *Successful Data Processing System Analysis*.

With respect to project definition (an organized effort to reach a *predefined* goal), it isn't until the end of the design phase that a project exists. Only then has the goal been defined in terms of system function and design. At this point, the *functional* and *design specifications* are *frozen*, and a project leader can be held to his *time*, *cost*, and *quality responsibilities*.

Consequently, from a strict point of view, everything we say about project management applies to system development only after functional and design specifications are frozen. However, functional specification and design of systems are sometimes a team effort. Much of what we say about managing projects in the construction phase also applies to leading teams engaged in functional specification and design of systems. Moreover, it's not uncommon for the project leader of a construction project to be the team leader of the functional specification and design efforts. Consequently, from time to time in this book, we say something about management responsibilities with respect to functional specification and design.

To freeze both functional and design specifications, each specification must be written and approved.

3.2.1.1 Functional Specifications. Functional specifications are approved by the user. In making this approval, the user attests that the functional specifications describe the system he wants.

Functional specifications are a voluminous document. The only way the user can approve this document is to have *participated actively* at a high level in its development. The question is, "How do you get the user actively involved at a high level?" We address this question in the chapter on directing activities.

Get your *user's approval* of the functional specifications in writing. If your user disagrees with the functional specifications, they must be rewritten until he agrees with them.

If your user expresses no disagreement with the functional specifications but doesn't sign off on them, bring this situation to your manager's attention. If he can't get the user to sign off on the functional specifications but wants system development to continue, he should sign off on the functional specifications. If neither your user nor your manager will sign off on the functional specifications, but your manager wants system development to continue, document your manager's decision in your next status report. If you aren't producing status reports, write a memo stating that the project has completed functional specification and is moving into design. Document your manager's decision in this memo.

3.2.1.2 Design Specifications.

Design specifications are approved by a *design review committee*. Every part of the company with an interest in the design of its systems is represented on this committee. Four such groups are

1. The System Development Department—The design review committee member from this department must attest to the technical acceptability of the design—does the system use available facilities efficiently and is the system flexible? In some organizations, this function is carried out by a *quality assurance group*.
2. The Computer Center—The member from this department must attest to the conformance of the system to computer center operating standards and facilities.
3. The Maintenance Group—This member must attest to the maintainability of the system.
4. The internal auditors—This member must attest that the design facilitates all audit functions.

If your system development department hasn't implemented the concept of a design review committee, form such a committee for your system, or have your design specifications reviewed and approved by people who would otherwise make up such a committee. For example, ask people in your department to review your design from the technical and maintainability points of view, ask a member of the computer center to review your design from his point of view, and ask an internal auditor to review your design for auditability.

3.2.1.3 Frozen Specifications.

To maximize the probability that, once frozen, functional and design specifications don't change, projects must be defined so that project duration is short—a year or less. For sizable systems, if a top-down approach is taken to functional specification and design, it's possible to spin off sub-systems not requiring more than a year of construction activity. The overall system can then be developed piecemeal, one sub-system at a time.

Freezing specifications doesn't mean that specifications can't be changed. It does mean, however, that you're going to base your plan, schedule, and cost estimate for system construction on approved specifications. If the specifications change, you have the right to adjust your plan, schedule, and estimate appropriately. Consequently, approval of functional specifications by the user means that he recognizes your right to adjust plans in response to specification change.

3.2.2 What The Phased Approach Means To The Project Leader

Thus far, we've discussed the phased approach to system development in terms of its function, namely, allowing you to complete your project within budget. This is the cost criterion on which your performance is judged. The phased approach to system development performs two other functions for you.

1. It allows you to complete your project on schedule. This is the time criterion on which your performance is judged.
2. It allows you to deliver a system that satisfies your user. This is the quality criterion on which your performance is judged.

The degree to which these performance criteria are relevant determines the way you use the phased approach to system development.

3.2.2.1 Full-Force Development. In some organizations, system development is a standardized activity. In these organizations, a phased approach to system development is spelled out in a system development methodology, and you're held to specified time, cost and quality criteria. In these circumstances, you deviate from the system development methodology at your own peril.

3.2.2.2 Fixed Time, Cost, And Quality Requirements. If no system development methodology exists but you're held to specific time, cost, and quality criteria, you must specify a phased approach to system development to be used on your project, and see that your user understands and conforms to it.

If the time, cost, and quality performance criteria to which you're held are less demanding, adjust your behavior accordingly. The next five sections of this chapter address various situations in which you may find yourself and describe the appropriate action to take in each situation.

3.2.2.3 Quality. Quality is something on which you can't compromise. No matter how loose your performance criteria, you must

1. Get your user as involved as you can in developing the functional specifications.
2. Document the functional specifications.
3. Get your user's agreement to the functional specifications, preferably in writing. However, if your organization doesn't require the user to sign off on functional specifications, and he shows reluctance to do so, don't make a fuss. Just do everything you can to see that he understands the functional specifications.
4. Get your design reviewed for technical quality, conformance to computer center requirements, and auditability.

5. Construct a maintainable system that conforms to the functional and design specifications.

3.2.2.4 Missing Cost Requirements.   You can be given time performance criteria with no mention of cost. If no one else thinks cost is a factor, don't hassle them, even though they're wrong. Instead, concentrate on your time requirements.

3.2.2.5 Time.   With respect to time, you must not commit to a deadline until the functional and design specifications are approved. You can, however, supply estimates on demand, but make clear that they're targets, not commitments.

If your construction deadline is rigid, you must use a *request for change procedure*, to prevent user requests for change to functional specifications from making your deadline unfeasible. A request for change form and the procedure for using it are described in Appendix A.

If your deadline is flexible, handle requests for change accordingly. Negotiate with your user and encourage him to limit his immediate requests for change to alterations that can't wait. Tell him you'll be happy to consider his other requests when the initial-system development is complete. Don't require a formal request for change procedure. If your user doesn't want to write up his requests for change, let him specify changes to you verbally. However, write them up and get him to review the write-ups to make sure you and he are communicating. Changes postpone system implementation. If things subsequently get nasty, your write-ups of requested changes document the reason for delay.

3.2.2.6 Modeling.   Sometimes an organization chooses to experiment with a system. Current nomenclature refers to this approach to system development as *modeling*. If modeling is chosen, two qualifications are in order:

1. Modeling doesn't relieve you from your quality responsibilities. Follow the procedures described in the section of this chapter on quality.
2. Be sure everyone understands that no specifications have been frozen and, thus, no commitments on time and cost can be made.

3.2.2.7 Where Project Leaders Go Wrong.   Project leaders err with respect to phased system development in terms of both omission and commission.

1. You're more lax than the situation calls for, in which case you're justifiably criticized for lack of performance.
2. Or you're more rigid than you need to be. You may think that, in so doing, you're being professional; but that won't be your user's reaction—he'll consider you a bureaucrat.

Be flexible—follow procedures that protect you as much as the situation calls for. If you have a user who makes it clear that he's going to hold you to commitments, use as much of the phased approach as needed to prevent him from making it impossible for you to meet your commitments. But if you have a user who prefers to keep his options open and not be firm on specifications, and who's willing to be understanding when specifications changes delay development, avoid wrapping him up in red tape.

The rest of this book assumes that you work in an environment in which functional and design specifications are frozen and in which you're held to, at least, time performance criteria.

3.2.3 Examples

Now let's apply the above principles to some examples. All six people working on your project are writing code. Are you in the construction phase?

There's insufficient information with which to answer this question. Whether you're in the construction phase has nothing to do with what the people on your team are doing. The construction phase is entered only when the functional and design specifications are frozen.

Your manager tells you that Charlie Brown has been promoted and that you're going to replace Charlie as project leader on the inventory system development project. Your manager tells you the development of the system has just entered the construction phase. What's your response to this statement?

Your response is, "If the project is in the construction phase, then approved functional and design specifications must exist. May I see them, please?" If these specifications can't be produced, you must respectfully submit that the project isn't in the construction phase.

3.3 THE ACCEPTANCE TEST

To plan the development of a system, you must know what constitutes the end of system development. An effective method for marking the end of system development is to have the system pass an acceptance test.

The user develops or approves the acceptance test. The user agrees, prior to running the test, that if the system passes the test, the system is accepted for use. Examples of acceptance tests are

1. Benchmarks—Specially developed tests.
2. Pilot tests—The system is installed on a limited basis.
3. Parallel operation—The system is installed but the previous system isn't discontinued.

In any case, it's necessary to specify, not only what the acceptance test will be, but also what constitutes successful completion of the test, which may be pre-determined results in the case of a benchmark or specification or what consti-tutes equivalent operation in the case of parallel operation.

Checking for equivalent results in parallel testing is a large-scale job for which adequate plans must be made. Typically, programs are used to automate the comparison. Decisions must be made concerning whether checked out totals are sufficient or whether details must be verified.

The acceptance test should include some demonstration of user personnel competence in use of the system. As a consequence, formal user training must be completed prior to the acceptance test, although the acceptance testing period is an excellent time to follow-up this formal training with simulated on-the-job experience. To conduct an effective training program, the user manual, input forms, specimen reports, and terminal dialogues must be available.

The proper time to develop the specifications for the acceptance test is at the time the functional specifications are being developed. Not only does such an approach satisfy the requirement that your user agree to the specifications of the acceptance test prior to running the test, but it also forces the kind of nuts and bolts thinking necessary to come up with functional specifications in which the user has confidence.

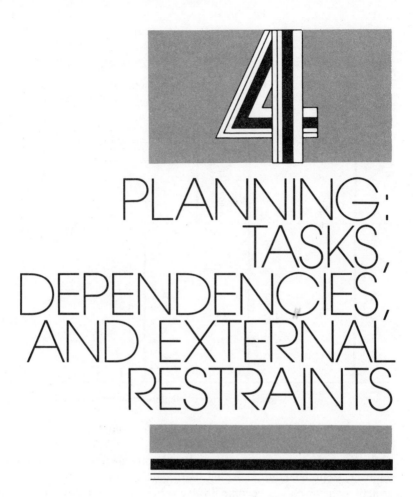

PLANNING: TASKS, DEPENDENCIES, AND EXTERNAL RESTRAINTS

Plans are necessary to

1. Project schedules.
2. Estimate costs.
3. Direct activities.

You, as a project leader, will develop plans at several points in system development. For example, suppose it has been decided to divide system development into four phases—initiation, functional specification, design, and construction; then you will develop five plans, as shown in Figure 4-1. The resources used in

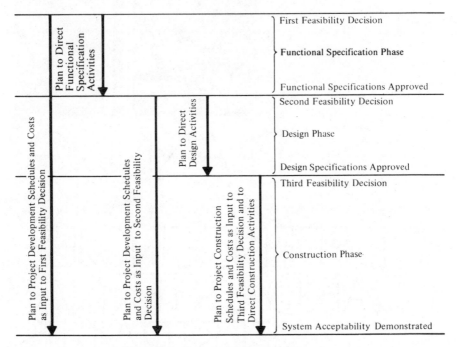

Figure 4-1. Project planning requirements.

system development include acquired *hardware* and *software, personnel,* and *computer time*.

On-line systems and the use of packaged software are becoming increasingly frequent. Consequently, managing the acquisition of hardware and software is an activity in which you become involved. However, we'll see that hardware and software acquisition management devolves into personnel management. Most of this book is devoted to the subject of managing personnel.

Computer time is a resource used in system development. Consequently, its use should be managed. This book, however, pays little attention to this topic, since few people are interested in it.

In summary, Chapters 4–7 deal mostly with personnel planning. We show how equipment and software acquisition planning devolves into personnel planning, and we say a few words about computer time planning.

Figure 4-1 shows the need to plan for five different jobs:

1. The functional specification, design, and construction of a system.
2. The functional specification of the system.
3. The design and construction of the system.
4. The design of the system.
5. The construction of the system.

A plan to do any of these jobs is developed as follows:

1. The *tasks* making up the job are listed.
2. The *dependency* between tasks is determined.
3. The *external restraints* under which the job must be performed are determined.
4. The time to do each task is estimated.
5. Personnel are assigned to the tasks.
6. Allowance for *contingencies* is made.

4.1 LISTING TASKS

The first step in plan development is to make a list of the tasks that must be done to complete a particular job. A task is a unit of work with a deliverable end product.

4.1.1 Functions

One approach to dividing a job into tasks is to look at the *functions* performed by the product of the job. For example, if the job is to build a house, the job can be divided into tasks on the basis of the functions performed by the house. Since a house provides shelter, it needs walls, a roof, and a floor. Depending on the climate, the house may also need insulation, a heating system, and an air conditioning system. People expect to use a house regardless of the natural lighting available and also expect to use appliances in a house. Consequently, a house needs an electrical system. People expect to use hot and cold running water in a house, together with bathing, washing, and toilet facilities. Thus, a house needs a plumbing and water heating system, sinks, tubs, showers, and toilets. People expect to be able to drive to their house and store their cars on the premises. Thus, a house needs a driveway, a parking space, and a garage. People accumulate personal property, which they expect to be able to store in their house. Thus, a house needs closets, an attic, and a basement. People expect their house to be attractive. Thus, landscaping is necessary. Also, some kind of exterior covering, such as paint or siding, is needed for a house. The list goes on. Thus, even lacking knowledge of how to build a house, we can divide the job into tasks by considering the functions performed by the house.

4.1.2 Activities

A second approach to dividing a job into tasks is to consider the *activities* that must be performed to do the job. For example, even if we've never done anything more serious in the kitchen than make a cup of instant coffee, we recognize that the job of preparing a dish consists of, at least, collecting the ingredients, mixing the ingredients, and cooking the mixture.

4.1.3 Functions and Activities

A third approach to dividing a job into tasks is to consider both the functions performed by the product of the job and the activities performed to do the job. For example, suppose the job is developing a system. Even without considering the nature of the particular system, we can say that a system performs the following functions: validates input data; updates records on the basis of the input data; does calculations; and produces reports. Here we've identified four functions—validation, updating, calculation, and report production. Suppose that in our example system each such function will be performed by a program. We then have four programs—a validation program, an update program, a calculation program, and a report producing program.

So much for functions. Now let's look at activities. Suppose the activities required to *develop a program* are

1. *Specify* the *program.*
2. *Structure* the *program.*
3. *Code* the program.
4. *Unit test* the program.

We can now construct a matrix of system functions and program development activities as shown in Figure 4-2. Here we've isolated 16 tasks (each represented by an element in the matrix) into which the job is divided. Sample tasks from this matrix are

1. Specify the validation program.
6. Structure the updating program.
11. Code the calculation program.
16. Unit test the report producing program.

To keep things simple, this example is abstract. In practice, however, a system includes functions in addition to the general functions listed in Figure 4-2. Moreover, system development consists of activities other than those involving program development. However, we hope we've made our point clear enough for you to consider both functions and activities when dividing a job into tasks.

In Figure 4-2, every element in the function-activity matrix represents a task. However, this isn't always the case. For example, suppose the job is to describe the way an organization's accounts receivable department operates. In addition, suppose that, in this organization, the accounts receivable operation performs the following six functions:

| | ACTIVITIES | | | |
FUNCTIONS	SPECIFY	STRUCTURE	CODE	UNIT TEST
VALIDATION	1	2	3	4
UPDATING	5	6	7	8
CALCULATION	9	10	11	12
REPORT PRODUCTION	13	14	15	16

Figure 4-2. Function-activity matrix.

1. Opening new accounts.
2. Checking credit.
3. Posting credit sales.
4. Posting cash receipts.
5. Issuing statements.
6. Making billing adjustments.

While this is an understatement of accounts receivable functions, the understatement is deliberate, to keep the example simple.

Let's further assume that we have five techniques—that is, five activities in which we can engage—to gather the information we need to develop our description of the accounts receivable operation.

1. Conduct interviews.
2. Study procedure manuals.
3. Study input forms.
4. Study record forms.
5. Study report forms.

Again, there are other information gathering techniques than those listed above. But for purposes of this example, let's keep it simple and restrict ourselves to this list.

Following the procedure we've learned, we use these functions and activities to construct the matrix shown in Figure 4-3. This matrix contains 30 elements. While it's possible that each element represents a task to be done in describing the accounts receivable operation, it's more likely that this isn't the case. Instead of being a tool for automatically identifying tasks, the function-activity matrix

| | ACTIVITIES | | | | |
FUNCTIONS	CONDUCT INTERVIEWS	STUDY PROCEDURE MANUALS	STUDY INPUT FORMS	STUDY RECORD FORMS	STUDY REPORT FORMS
OPENING NEW ACCOUNTS					
CHECKING CREDIT					
POSTING CREDIT SALES					
POSTING CASH RECEIPTS					
ISSUING STATEMENTS					
MAKING ADJUSTMENTS					

Figure 4-3. Function-activity matrix.

is more commonly used to methodically determine which elements are tasks and which are empty combinations of functions and activities.

Thus, in the case of the matrix in Figure 4-3, there may be a procedure manual that describes how to open accounts, post credit sales and cash receipts, issue statements, and make adjustments. A study of this manual may be all we need to understand how these functions are carried out. On the other hand, to determine how to check credit, it may be necessary to conduct an interview. All of the functions involve the use of customer records. Moreover, opening new accounts, posting credit sales and cash receipts, and making adjustments involve the use of input forms. Issuing statements, on the other hand, involves producing reports. Consequently the tasks described by the function-activity matrix shown in Figure 4-3 may be as shown in Figure 4-4. In Figure 4-4, a matrix element represents a task if it contains an X.

4.1.4 Summary

When dividing a job into tasks, think in terms of both functions and activities. Ultimately, you may decide, for example, that thinking in terms of activities alone results in a task list adequate for your purposes. But don't leap to this conclusion prematurely—investigate the functions first.

	ACTIVITIES				
FUNCTIONS	CONDUCT INTERVIEWS	STUDY PROCEDURE MANUALS	STUDY INPUT FORMS	STUDY RECORD FORMS	STUDY REPORT FORMS
OPENING NEW ACCOUNTS	–	X	X	X	–
CHECKING CREDIT	X	–	–	X	–
POSTING CREDIT SALES	–	X	X	X	–
POSTING CASH RECEIPTS	–	X	X	X	–
ISSUING STATEMENTS	–	X	–	X	X
MAKING ADJUSTMENTS	–	X	X	X	–

Figure 4-4. Function-activity matrix.

Thus far, we've given examples of how (when thinking in terms of functions and activities) a function-activity matrix can be an aid. Consistent use of such a matrix isn't a bad idea since it's methodical and may identify tasks you would have otherwise overlooked. However, we don't want to be rigid. Thus, when the combinations of functions and activities aren't complex, construction of a matrix may not be necessary. Just thinking in terms of functions and activities may be sufficient to arrive at a task list.

Moreover, dividing a job into tasks isn't usually as clear-cut as our presentation of the subject may lead you to believe. For example, it's typically necessary to use several function-activity matrices to list the tasks making up a job. Thus, as we pointed out in our example of developing a system, the function-activity matrix we constructed for program development represents only one group of tasks in the job.

4.1.5 Example

We're now going to develop an example which illustrates the tasks making up a job. In developing an example, there's a conflict between developing an example that's complicated but realistic and developing an example that emphasizes major points but is simplified and unrealistic. Faced with this dilemma, we opted for an example that's graphic but simplified.

The job is to construct an assembler, linker, and loader for computer X. The functional and design specifications for this software package have been developed and approved. A design decision calls for the programs to be written in computer X assembly code. Consequently, it's decided to develop a boot assembler that will run on computer Y, a computer with an already existing software system. The boot assembler will run on computer Y, accept computer X source code, and produce computer X object code, but will be written in computer Y source code, so it can be assembled and run with the already existing software available in computer Y. The system to be constructed thus performs the following functions:

1. Boot assemble.
2. Load.
3. Assemble.
4. Link.

Up to now the reality of the example hasn't been degraded by simplification.

Now let's suppose that the following activities must be performed to get the job done:

1. Code.
2. Assemble.
3. Develop unit test data.
4. Perform unit test.
5. Perform *link test*.

In this activity list we've simplified the example. Thus, activities such as preparing program specifications, writing the user manual, and developing the link test have been left out.

The function-activity matrix for this project is as shown in Figure 4-5. The task list can be read from this matrix as follows:

1. Code boot assembler.
2. Code loader.
3. Code assembler.
4. Code linker.
5. Assemble boot assembler.
6. Assemble loader.
7. Assemble assembler.
8. Assemble linker.

Functions \ Activities	Code	Assemble	Develop Unit Test Data	Perform Unit Test	Perform Link Test
Boot Assembler	X	X	X	X	—
Loader	X	X	X	X	X
Assembler	X	X	X	X	X
Linker	X	X	X	X	X

Figure 4-5. Function-activity matrix for the software package construction project.

9. Develop boot assembler unit test data.
10. Develop loader unit test data.
11. Develop assembler unit test data.
12. Develop linker unit test data.
13. Unit test boot assembler.
14. Unit test loader.
15. Unit test assembler.
16. Unit test linker.
17. Link test.

The link-test task in the above list accounts for three of the X's in the function-activity matrix in Figure 4-5, since the loader, assembler, and linker are all involved in this activity.

4.2 DETERMINING TASK DEPENDENCY

Typically when doing a job, some tasks must be finished before others can be started. For example, a program must be coded before it can be compiled, it must be compiled before it can be unit tested, and unit test data for the program must also be developed before the program can be unit tested. Also, in our software construction project, the boot assembler must be unit tested before the loader, assembler, or linker can be assembled. In addition, the assembler and linker can't be unit tested until they can be loaded, and since it's the loader which loads the assembler and linker, it follows that the loader must be unit tested before the assembler or linker can be unit tested.

The fact that one task must be completed before another can be started is referred to as *task dependency*. Thus, if a program must be coded before it can be compiled, the task of program compilation is said to be dependent on the task of program coding.

The concept of task dependency brings up the topic of PERT/CPM. In this book, we use some PERT/CPM concepts. Consequently, the first thing to do is learn some PERT/CPM terminology.

4.2.1 PERT/CPM

The name, PERT/CPM, is a combination of two acronyms, PERT and CPM. The combination indicates that the PERT/CPM method is an amalgam of two independently developed techniques. (The differences in technique are no longer significant.) As a consequence, the PERT/CPM technique is an integrated method, for contending with task dependency, that recognizes its multiple origins in its name.

PERT is an acronym for *Program Evaluation Review Technique*. Perhaps a better name would have been Project Evaluation Review Technique, but this is the wisdom of hindsight.

PERT evolved out of work done by the United States Navy Special Projects Office, which in 1958, set up a team to devise a means of dealing with the planning and subsequent control of complex work. By October of 1958, the method had been sufficiently developed to allow its use in the Fleet Ballistic Missiles program, where it was applied to the development of the Polaris missile.

CPM is an acronym for *Critical Path Method*. This technique was used by Du Pont, also beginning in 1958, to schedule and control large projects.

The use of PERT/CPM begins with a list of the tasks making up a job. In Figure 4-6, we show a list of tasks for building a house. Again, for purposes of clarity, this list is simplified. (More tasks than those listed are involved in building a house.) However, let's assume that the tasks in Figure 4-6 are the only tasks involved in building a house.

The dependency between the tasks listed in Figure 4-6 is shown in Figure 4-7. Figure 4-7 shows that the foundation must be poured before the frame can be erected, the frame must be erected before either the roofing or wiring can be done, and both the roofing and wiring must be done before the walls can be plastered. Figure 4-7 is a graphic representation of task dependency and is called a *network*.

POUR FOUNDATION
ERECT FRAME
DO ROOFING
DO WIRING
PLASTER WALLS

Figure 4-6. Tasks for building a house.

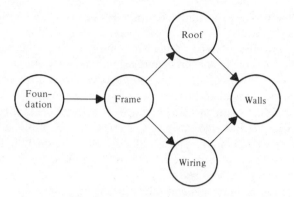

Figure 4-7. Task dependency.

Now let's learn a few PERT/CPM terms used to describe the tasks in a network. Look at the *foundation task* in Figure 4-7. All the other tasks in the network are *successors* of the foundation task—that is, none of the other tasks can start until the foundation task is completed. However, the only *immediate successor* of the foundation task is the frame task—that is, once the foundation task is completed, only the frame task can start.

Now look at the walls task in Figure 4-7. All the other tasks in the network are *predecessors* of the walls task—that is, all the other tasks must be completed before the walls task can start. However, only two of the tasks (roofing and wiring) are *immediate predecessors* of the walls task. These two tasks are the only immediate predecessors of the walls task, because only the walls task is the immediate successor of both the roof and wiring tasks.

As in Figure 4-7, networks are depicted with circles and *arrows.* The circles are referred to as nodes or *bubbles*.

There are two types of networks. One type depicts the tasks inside the bubbles, as in Figure 4-7. In this type of network, the arrows represent the dependency between tasks. We refer to this type of network as a *task-on-bubble network*, or precedent networking.

The other type of network depicts the tasks on arrows, and is called an arrow diagram, or a *task-on-arrow network*. Another name for this type of network is event networking. The task-on-arrow network was developed prior to the task-on-bubble network.

In this book, we adopt the task-on-bubble type of network, as shown in Figure 4-7. This is in keeping with the current trend.

As shown in Figure 4-7, to conform to PERT/CPM practice, a network must have a single *start task* and a single *end task*. In Figure 4-7, the foundation task is the start task, and the walls task the end task.

The definition of a project as work directed toward a predefined goal guarantees that a network has a single end task. However, when starting a project, it may be possible to begin several tasks at once. For example, in constructing a system, it's possible to start writing programs, developing the link test, and developing the file conversion procedure, simultaneously. In such a case, the need for a single start task can be met by introducing an arbitrary task named start, which is the immediate predecessor of all the beginning tasks. The alternative is to dispense with the single start-task requirement. Since we're not going to use PERT/CPM rigorously in this book, we adopt this alternative.

Also, because we're not going to use PERT/CPM rigorously in this book, we don't use the PERT/CPM term network to refer to the networks we construct. Instead, we call them *bubble charts*.

So much for the components and relationships that make up a bubble chart. Let's now turn our attention to the procedures for determining the dependency between tasks.

4.2.2 Procedures

To determine task dependency in any particular case, a knowledge of the *source* of task dependencies is helpful. Given this knowledge, an *immediate predecessor task list* is used to ferret out dependencies. The source of task dependencies and the immediate predecessor task list are discussed in the following two sections.

4.2.2.1 The Source of Dependencies. One source of task dependencies is the activities that must be performed to do the job. For example, your knowledge of how to develop systems tells you that assembling a program is dependent on coding it and that unit testing a program is dependent on both assembling the program and developing unit test data.

A second source of task dependencies is the function of each task making up the job. Thus:

1. The function of the boot assembler tells you that assembly of the loader, assembler, and linker are dependent on unit testing the boot assembler.
2. The function of the loader tells you that unit testing the assembler and linker are dependent on unit testing the loader.

A third area in which to look for dependencies is the approach you take to the job. For example, if you decide to use the assembler to develop unit test data for the linker, then development of this test data is dependent on unit testing the assembler. On the other hand, if you decide to develop unit test data for the linker from scratch, then this task is independent of unit testing the assembler.

4.2.2.2 The Immediate Predecessor Task List. Construction of an immediate predecessor task list begins with creating a list of the tasks making up

Task	Immediate Predecessors
1. CODE BOOT ASSEMBLER	—
2. CODE LOADER	—
3. CODE ASSEMBLER	—
4. CODE LINKER	—
5. ASSEMBLE BOOT ASSEMBLER	1
6. ASSEMBLE LOADER	2, 13
7. ASSEMBLE ASSEMBLER	3, 13
8. ASSEMBLE LINKER	4, 13
9. DEVELOP BOOT ASSEMBLER TEST DATA	—
10. DEVELOP LOADER TEST DATA	—
11. DEVELOP ASSEMBLER TEST DATA	—
12. DEVELOP LINKER TEST DATA	—
13. UNIT TEST BOOT ASSEMBLER	5, 9
14. UNIT TEST LOADER	6, 10
15. UNIT TEST ASSEMBLER	7, 11, 14
16. UNIT TEST LINKER	8, 12, 14
17. LINK TEST	15, 16

Figure 4-8. Immediate predecessor task list.

the job. The task list for our software project is shown in Figure 4-8. The first step in developing an immediate predecessor task list is to number the tasks in the list, as has been done in Figure 4-8.

The second step is to enter, following each task in the list, the numbers of the immediate predecessors of the task. Thus, the first task in the task list is to code the boot assembler, which has no predecessors. This fact is indicated by entering a dash in the immediate predecessors column in Figure 4-8.

The immediate predecessor of assembling the boot assembler is coding the boot assembler; therefore, a one (the task number of coding the boot assembler) is entered in the immediate predecessors column next to assembling the boot assembler. Assembling the loader has two immediate predecessors—coding the loader and unit testing the boot assembler. The numbers of these immediate predecessor tasks are two and 13; so two and 13 are entered in the immediate predecessors column next to assembling the loader. Identifying the other immediate predecessors in Figure 4-8 follows the same procedure.

Construction of an immediate predecessor task list can't guarantee that, after its construction, you'll have identified all task dependencies. However, such a list assures that you've systematically contemplated each task with regard to its immediate predecessors, and such an approach is sufficient enough to recommend its use. Using the list enables you to recognize more immediate predecessors than you would otherwise.

4.2.3 The Bubble Chart

Once an immediate predecessor task list is developed, a bubble chart can be constructed mechanically from the immediate predecessor task list. The procedure is as follows.

In Figure 4-8, coding the boot assembler, task one, is the immediate predecessor of assembling the boot assembler. Therefore, in the bubble chart, there should be an arrow running from the code-the-boot-assembler bubble to the assemble-the-boot-assembler bubble, as in Figure 4-9.

Similarly, coding the loader and unit testing the boot assembler, tasks two and 13, are the immediate predecessors of assembling the loader. Thus, there should be an arrow running from the code-the-loader bubble to the assemble-the-loader bubble and also an arrow running from the unit-test-the-boot-assembler bubble to the assemble-the-loader bubble. Such is the case in Figure 4-9.

When all arrows have been drawn, as called for by the immediate predecessor task list in Figure 4-8, the bubble chart in Figure 4-9 emerges. On the first try, the bubble chart won't come out as neatly as the one shown in Figure 4-9. But a couple of iterations to put the bubbles in convenient positions produces a readable bubble chart.

Since a bubble chart can be mechanically constructed from an immediate predecessor task list, there's no information in the bubble chart that is not already present in the immediate predecessor task list. So why construct a bubble chart?

There are four reasons for converting your immediate predecessor task list to a bubble chart:

1. Developing a bubble chart slows you down and forces you to spend more time thinking about task dependencies than you might otherwise. As a result, you're likely to recognize dependencies you might otherwise have overlooked.
2. Planning isn't a one-time thing. As development on your project proceeds, progress will deviate from your original plan. It then becomes necessary to modify your plan to retain your best posture toward your project goal. At the time you modify your plan, you'll want to refresh your memory about task dependencies. A bubble chart is a clear, concise method for documenting these dependencies for future reference.
3. After you develop your plan, you must get your manager's approval of it, since he supplies the personnel that, both of you agree, are needed to meet your goal. In getting his approval, one of the things you must convince him of is the dependency that exists between the tasks making up your job. Have you ever negotiated with the manager who says, "Hmm, so you need three people for a year. That's too long. Let's put six people on it and get it done in six months," when the dependency between tasks dictates that a year is

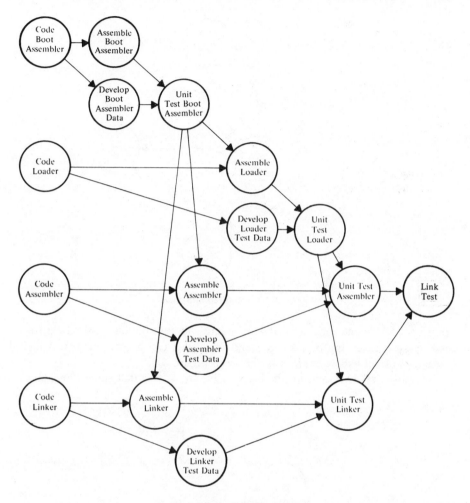

Figure 4-9. Bubble chart.

as soon as you can get the job done no matter how many people are working on it? A bubble chart is an effective presentation technique for getting across your task dependency situation.

4. Constructing a bubble chart facilitates the detection of certain errors in identifying task dependencies that don't show clearly in an immediate predecessor task list.

One type of error a bubble chart may help you detect is the lack of a single end task. An example of a bubble chart with multiple end-tasks is shown in Figure 4-10. One possible reason for the lack of a single end task is that a de-

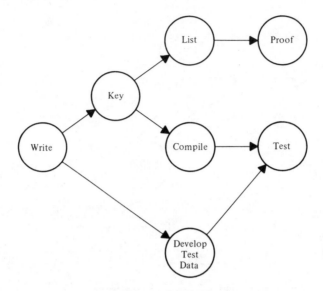

Figure 4-10. Multiple end-tasks.

pendency has been overlooked. Perhaps there's an installation requirement stating that a code listing be proofed before the code can be compiled, in which case the correct bubble chart is as shown in Figure 4-11.

Another possible reason for the error in Figure 4-10 is that superfluous tasks

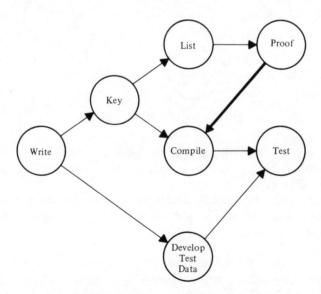

Figure 4-11. Corrected bubble chart.

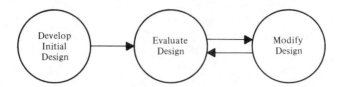

Figure 4-12. Loop of tasks.

have been included in the task list. It could be that, since the compiler proofs the code as it reads the code, having the programmer proof a code listing is unnecessary. If this is the case, eliminating the list and proof tasks from the bubble chart in Figure 4-10 corrects the bubble chart.

A second type of error that a bubble chart may help detect is a *loop*. An example of a loop of tasks is shown in Figure 4-12. The loop in this figure is the simplest loop possible. More complex loops have several tasks making up the loop. The common characteristic is that each task in a loop is a predecessor of itself.

One way out of a loop is to divide the activity into phases—initial design, intermediate design, and final design, as shown in Figure 4-13. Or if the activity, such as design, is an interactive, feedback activity in which evaluation and modification occur in a rapid, dynamic, unpredictable way, then the loop is eliminated by subsuming the three activities of initial design development, design evaluation, and design modification within a single task, named "develop design."

Converting an immediate predecessor task list into a bubble chart also exposes *superfluous dependencies.* An example of a superfluous dependency is shown in Figure 4-14, where the dependency of task *C* on task *A* is superfluous, since

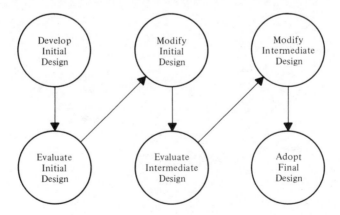

Figure 4-13. Dividing tasks into phases.

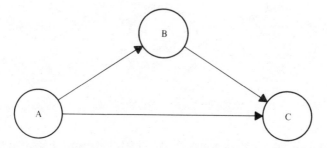

Figure 4-14. Superfluous dependency.

C is also dependent on task *B*, and *B* is dependent on *A*. Superfluous dependencies aren't errors but can be discarded.

A rigorous use of PERT/CPM requires that tasks be defined in such a way
that no task can begin until all its immediate predecessors are complete. This
is a difficult requirement to meet. In many cases, a task can't be completed until
its immediate predecessors are complete, but it can be started. For example,
when developing a system, it's not possible to complete link testing the system
until all programs in the system are developed. However, if development of the
programs is scheduled properly, it may be possible to begin link testing before
all the programs have been developed. The PERT/CPM solution is to subdivide
the tasks into smaller subtasks. For example, instead of having just one task
named "link test," as shown in Figure 4-15, you can use the approach shown
in Figure 4-16. Here the link test task is preceded by subsystem test tasks, which
represent the aspects of link testing that can be done before program development is complete.

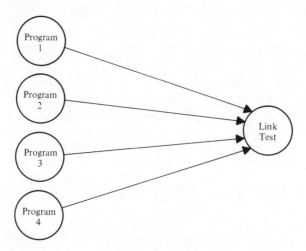

Figure 4-15. No subtasks.

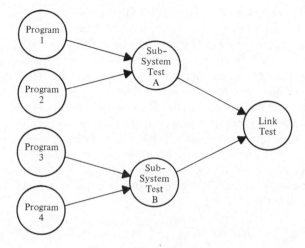

Figure 4-16. Using subtasks.

The approach shown in Figure 4-16 is required if PERT/CPM techniques are to be used to compute job finish times. However, this isn't what we're going to use a bubble chart for. Consequently, we suggest that you not wrestle with the problem that the Figure 4-16 approach is designed to solve. Instead, relax the PERT/CPM requirement. Your bubble charts should show tasks whose *completion* is dependent on the completion of their immediate predecessors. This is as refined as you have to get in identifying dependencies for planning.

4.3 DETERMINING EXTERNAL RESTRAINTS

Project activities are carried out in an environment that places limits on when and how these activities can be performed. We refer to these limits as external restraints.

To develop a plan, you must know what your job's external restraints are. But because you contend with external restraints well after a plan is developed, and because they're beyond your control, the best you can do is get commitments, from those who control the external restraints, as to what they'll be.

Three classes of external restraints are as follows:

1. Deadlines—You infrequently have difficulty getting commitments regarding deadlines. People to whom you're obligated to deliver products are generally explicit as to when they must have the products and display resoluteness concerning these commitments as time passes.
2. Delivery dates—It may be necessary for someone to deliver a product to you before you can get beyond a certain point in the development of your system. For example, in our software project, we can't do any unit testing of the

loader until we get access to the new computer or a facsimile thereof. Thus, availability of a prototype in an appropriate time frame, or existence of a simulator, becomes an external restraint on our project.

3. Turnaround rates—System development requires some repetitive services. Unit test shots are an example of this type of service. Here the service is always available; therefore, the problem isn't one of delivery dates. Instead, it's turnaround that concerns you. For example, given the actual number of hours it takes to unit test a program, the turnaround on unit test shots determines the *elapsed time* over which the *actual time* is spread. For example, if turnaround is essentially instantaneous, actual time and elapsed time are equivalent. However, if turnaround is 24 hours, a person may be able to spend an average of only half of each day in a unit test mode. Elapsed time is then double the actual time.

The external restraints on which your plans are based must be part of your plans.

1. Deadlines appear on your schedule.
2. Turnaround rates are enumerated in a list that becomes part of your plan documentation.
3. Delivery dates are put on your bubble chart.

The external restraint concerning availability of the new computer is shown in the bubble chart in Figure 4-17. Use a symbol, other than a circle, to represent external restraints, so they can be distinguished from your tasks.

External restraints other than deadlines, delivery dates, and turnaround rates exist. For example, your budget is an external restraint. We talk about these other external restraints from time to time in the following chapters.

4.4 EQUIPMENT AND SOFTWARE ACQUISITION PLANNING

Earlier we said that equipment and software acquisition planning devolves into personnel planning. We've now come far enough in the development of the planning process to demonstrate this point.

Suppose the job is to select a piece of equipment or software. The tasks making up the job might be as follows:

1. Determine functional requirements.
2. Identify available vendors.
3. Collect information on vendors and their products.
4. Analyze the collected information.
5. Select vendor.

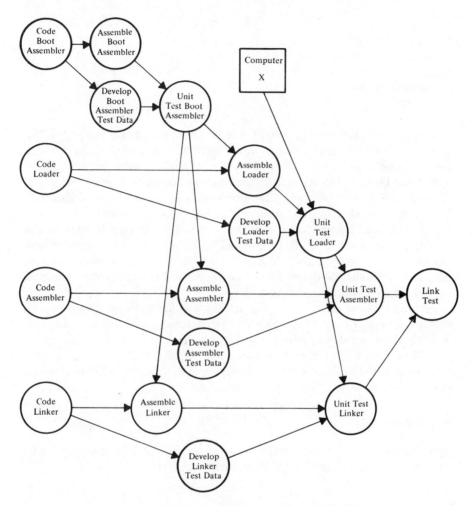

Figure 4-17. Bubble chart with external restraints.

As can be seen by inspecting the above list, there's no difference between this set of tasks and any other we've been developing. We must determine the dependencies between tasks, estimate the time to do each task, assign personnel to the tasks, and allow for contingencies—just as in any other plan.

Suppose the vendor and product have been selected and the job is to put the product into production. Specifically, suppose the product is a terminal. The activities making up this job might be as follows:

1. Do site survey.
2. Install wiring.

3. Prepare site.
4. Train operators.
5. Modify operating system.
6. Accept delivery.
7. Install terminal.
8. Go live.

In this list, the activities have been phrased in terms that make them look like tasks. However, one, and maybe more, of these activities aren't tasks. Instead, they're external restraints. The activity that's unquestionably an external restraint is the accept delivery activity. You may be accepting delivery, but you're doing it on a delivery date negotiated between you and the vendor. You don't have complete control over the determination of this date. Similarly, if the wiring is to be installed by a crew, you either contract with outside your organization, or negotiate with inside your organization, you don't have complete control over this activity, either. Then, it also becomes an external restraint. Similarly, any other of the above activities that are not under your complete control are also external restraints.

But in the case of each activity, the activity is either an external restraint, for which you negotiate, or a task, to which you assign personnel under your control. Thus, we see that acquiring a piece of equipment or software consists of planning for tasks and external restraints.

So there's nothing new here. Equipment and software acquisition planning devolves into personnel planning.

4.5 EXAMPLE

Specifications for a payroll system are given in Appendix B. In Appendix C, we develop a task list and bubble chart for this project.

PLANNING: TIME ESTIMATING AND PERSONNEL ASSIGNMENT

5.1 TIME ESTIMATING

To talk about task time estimating we must distinguish between actual and elapsed time. Let's suppose we estimate that it will take a person, working full-time on a task, ten days to complete the task. This is an estimate of actual time. To distinguish between actual and elapsed time, we express actual time in units known as *person days*. Thus, in the case at hand, we say it will take ten person days to complete the task.

If the person can work full-time on the task, then our actual time estimate is also an elapsed time estimate. We estimate that the person will complete the task in ten calendar days. Thus, we see that elapsed time is measured in *calendar days*.

But even in this simple case, there's a problem. If the person works only five days a week, full-time, then ten person days is equivalent to a minimum of 12 calendar days and may be equivalent to 14 calendar days depending on which day of the week the person starts work.

What we're seeing here is the transformation of an actual time estimate into an elapsed time estimate by taking external restraints into consideration. In this case, the external restraint is the five day workweek.

We eliminate the impact of the workweek on the relation between actual and elapsed time by using a calendar with weeks consisting of five days each. In the rest of this book, we use such a calendar.

Let's now suppose that, because of some external restraint such as work demands, a person can work only half-time on the task we estimated would take ten person days to complete; then roughly speaking, the person will complete the task in 20 calendar days. However, this isn't completely true. The need to frequently put the task aside and come back to it imposes an added restraint on the worker. Each time he comes back to the task, some time has to be spent getting reoriented to the task—where the work left off, what problems were going to be tackled next, etc. Consequently, it may take the person 21 or 22 elapsed days to complete the task.

The conversion of actual time into elapsed time can also go the other way. For example, you may decide that ten calendar days is too much time to spend on the task. Consequently, you decide to assign two people to the task. Theoretically, this reduces the elapsed time to five calendar days, since two people divided into ten person days gives five calendar days. However, elapsed time won't be confined to five calendar days, since two people working on one task must coordinate with each other. This coordination takes time. Consequently, it may take six or seven calendar days for the two people to complete the task.

Such thoughts lead to the conclusion that there's some upper limit to the number of people who can be assigned to a task with a resulting reduction in elapsed time. Beyond this point, coordinating activities become the dominant factor influencing elapsed time. With the addition of more personnel, elapsed time starts to increase rather than continuing to decrease. For an amusing exposition of this point, complete with allegorical illustrations of dinosaurs trapped in tar pits, see The Mythical Man Month, by Frederick P. Brooks, Jr. (Addison-Wesley, 1975). For a more serious discussion of the topic, see *Controlling Software Projects* pp. 178–184.

In this book, when we use the term, task time, we're referring to actual task time. When we wish to distinguish between actual task time and elapsed task time we'll use the terms, actual task time and elapsed task time, explicitly.

The procedure for determining elapsed task time is as follows:

1. Estimate actual task time.
2. Extend this estimate by the external restraints impinging on the task to arrive at an elapsed time estimate.

Thus, when we're talking about estimating task time, we're referring to estimating actual task time. Estimating the time to do a task can't be done without considering the person assigned to the task, since task time is a function of the *capability* of the person assigned. Nevertheless, we're going to separate the two subjects analytically by stating that one factor determining task time is the capability of the person assigned to the task. We're then going to postpone the subject of assigning personnel to tasks until we finish discussing time estimating.

The other factor influencing task time is the *complexity* of the task. Thus, when doing time estimating, keep two factors in mind:

1. The complexity of the task.
2. The capability of the person assigned to the task.

Up to now, the discussion of time estimating is clear. From this point on, however, things become murky. To combat this murkiness we divide the topic into two subjects. First we discuss what time estimating isn't, and then we tackle the question of how to do time estimating.

5.1.1 What Time Estimating Isn't

Although our time estimating techniques are minimal, we nevertheless want to do the best job possible. Because techniques are minimal, the danger exists that we'll slip into some technique that isn't really time estimating, under the delusion that we're doing time estimating. To avoid this trap, it pays to know what time estimating isn't, so you can avoid these psuedo-techniques.

Tom DeMarco (1978) gives what we feel is the best description of what time estimating isn't (pp. 336, 337). What follows is a lightly edited version of DeMarco's points.

Suppose . . . your boss rushes in with this request:

> "Quick, give me your estimate for how long it's going to take you working full time without help to do such and such between now and this time next year."

If you respond, "One year," your boss will conclude that you are a splendid estimator and depart, well pleased. But you have not estimated anything. You have only regurgitated.

Rule 1: Estimating is different from regurgitating.

We are often called upon to regurgitate in the guise of estimating. Sometimes our superiors are subtler in letting us know what the "right answer" is. They might use an arched eyebrow or a soto-voce hint. But if there *is* a right answer and everyone knows it, then you are not even being asked to estimate, but to regurgitate.

Suppose you refuse to regurgitate like a good fellow, and respond by saying, "It can't be done by this time next year. I need 14 months." You are . . . still not estimating. [You're] negotiating.

Rule 2: Estimating is different from negotiating.

If you negotiate instead of estimate, you have started off on the wrong foot. Your sin, however, is not nearly as serious as if you first estimate and *then* negotiate. When you come up with your best estimate of an unknown, it makes no sense at all to let someone, namely your boss, make a counter offer.

Rule 3: Estimations are not subject to bargaining.

It is well to cultivate an air of stunned disbelief to greet any attempt at bargaining. At the very least, you are obliged to tell whoever makes the counter offer that the estimate is now his.

Suppose your boss asks you to . . . "Make us up a schedule for three people to complete the Python-X project in one year." If you lay out a schedule showing duration of analysis, design, and coding, you are still not estimating—you are dividing.

Rule 4: Estimating is different from dividing a fixed duration into component parts.
So don't regurgitate, negotiate, *or* divide.

5.1.2 Time Estimating Techniques

There are three time estimating techniques:

1. *Professional judgment*.
2. The *historical technique*.
3. Use of *standards*.

We discuss each below.

5.1.2.1 Professional Judgment.

With this method, a person relies on the memory of his past experiences, the experiences of his acquaintances, and his unformulated impressions of the importance of various factors to come up with an estimate. For instance, a person experienced in the applications area for which the estimates are being made may be able to come up with relatively precise estimates. The disadvantages of this technique are

1. It can't be used unless you have access to someone experienced in the applications area in which you're working.
2. The technique is inclined to give insufficient consideration to variations in capability. That is, the estimator tends to come up with an estimate of how long it would take him to do the task regardless of who's going to be assigned the task.

However, one thing is for sure. Independent of the advantages and disadvantages of professional judgment, in the absence of the ability to use the historical technique or standards, professional judgment is the only time estimating technique available.

5.1.2.2 Historical Technique.   The question is: How long will it take person *A* to do task *X?* The approach is to find some other task (task *Y*) that has been done in the past, that resembles task *X* as closely as possible and that was done by a person, (person B) who has capabilities in common with person *A*. The time it took person *B* to do task *Y* is then adjusted on the basis of the differences between tasks *X* and *Y*, and the capabilities of persons *A* and *B*. This adjusted time is used as the estimate of the time it will take person *A* to do task *X*. The drawback to the historical approach is that few installations have enough reliable historical data to allow use of the technique. We investigate this topic in further detail in the next section.

5.1.2.3 Use Of Standards.   A standard involves the methodical assignment of values to various characteristics of a task and to the person assigned to the task. These values are then combined in a standard way to yield an estimate. The attraction of standards is that they're the only technique that promises the possibility of systematically improving estimating skills. Only the standards method spells out a procedure for arriving at a time estimate. Consequently, it alone offers the possibility that repeated comparison of estimated against actual time will reveal inadequacies in the procedure, which can then be refined.

5.1.2.3.1 Characteristics of Standards.   The best book on time estimating standards is DeMarco's *Controlling Software Projects* (1982). De Marco is a Yourdonite, a group of people that Ed Yourdon has gathered around him. These people study the work of researchers in the field of data processing and translate these researchers' findings into words that are more readily understood by data processing practioners. So if you want to emerse yourself in the topic of time estimating standards, *Controlling Software Projects* is the place to start.

The concept of time estimating standards is an application of the management information principle that collecting data on performance enables you to make performance predicting generalizations. By collecting data on the predicted performance, you can determine the accuracy of your predictions by comparing actual performance with predicted performance. Such a comparison may lead you to modify your generalizations to more accurately predict performance; thus, the cycle starts again. Over time, using such an approach should improve the predictive capabilities of your generalizations.

This is true as long as the data collected is *reliable* and *consistent*.

5.1.2.3.1.1 Reliability. Data collected regarding time usage is reliable if it reflects the usage of time as it actually occurred. Many installations have *time reporting systems*, although the data collected by these systems is, in most cases, not very reliable. Most time reporting systems are one of two types:

1. They feed the payroll system. The primary rule here is: put anything you want on your time card but be sure it adds up to 40 hours.
2. They feed so-called project management systems. We've several things to say about such systems.
   a. They're misnamed. They're not project management systems—that is, they aren't systems that manage projects. Instead, they're time reporting systems that have the ability to generate variance reports.
   b. We understand why they're misnamed. If we were selling such a package, we'd call it a project management system, too. After all, how many prospects think they have a time reporting problem? This is a different question than, "How many installations have a time reporting problem?" to which the answer must be, "Most."
   c. The problem arises when management tries to use the system according to its name. Thus, instead of being used to refine estimating techniques, variance reports are used to evaluate performance. It's sad to see that, of all the ways to evaluate performance, management chooses the least effective—the time report.
   d. The consequence is that personnel see their time cards as pawns in the game of getting ahead or staying even. As a result, the data collected on a time card is more a reflection of an employee's ingenuity than how he used his time.

DeMarco (1982, p. 136) is on the mark with his solution to the problem of misusing time reports. The following, again edited, is what he has to say.

When time is charged to a task, the worker must feel confident that the accounting is for a historical record only. The way to effect this feeling is to make time reporting the responsibility of people who're separated from all other aspects of management. Call these people the *metrics group*.

The metrics group collects records on a regular basis, usually weekly. Metrics group members meet with each project worker to find out how the intervening time has been spent, and the metrics group members decide on the allocation of time to tasks. The worker has no knowledge of how time is charged, time used to date, or time remaining. The worker isn't obliged to account for the full work period. (Also, we'd add, if the project member worked overtime, he should account for it.)

Time records thus collected are confidential to the metrics group. Managers are sometimes offended at the idea that information is purposely kept from them by policy of their company. IRS agents are equally offended that the Census Bureau won't share income data with them. In both cases, the rationale is the same. The data can't be collected if it's not protected. If the data is useful, then protecting it should be considered part of the price of collecting it.

If you're not willing to collect time usage data as DeMarco recommends, then forget about building a database on which to predict time usage; you won't be successful. Besides, you don't need a time usage database to control your project and evaluate personnel performance anyhow; *checkpoints* and *quality of performance* are the tools here. We discuss both in the part of the book dealing with directing activities.

5.1.2.3.1.2 Consistency. If the data collected regarding time usage are consistent, then each time a project member reports that he's spent some time on a task, every other project member in the same situation would make the same report. Consistency is enhanced when tasks are

1. Defined objectively.
2. Standardized.

5.1.2.3.1.2.1 Objective Task Definition. Consistency in assigning time to tasks depends on an objective definition of tasks. Objectivity is achieved by defining tasks in terms of a deliverable end product. In this way, a project member knows that, if he's working on the development of a deliverable end product, then the task defined by this deliverable end product is the one to which his time should be charged. He also knows that, until the end product is delivered, he hasn't completed the task.

Up to some limit, the shorter the time required to complete a task, the more precise the estimates based on past performance will be. Consequently, an effort to define tasks in detail has a payoff (again up to some limit). A good rule of thumb is that each task should be such that a person working on it full-time would need at least a week, but not more than a month, to complete it.

However, the requirement to define tasks in terms of deliverable end products is prime. As DeMarco says (1982, p.137):

> Deliverable-oriented project modeling may yield some overly large [tasks] . . . But further dividing those [tasks] into components that produce no discernible product is to invest precious effort in an illusion of detailed planning.

5.1.2.3.1.2.2 Task Standardization. From the point of view of time estimating, the advantage of standardizing task definitions is that such a step creates categories in which time usage data can be collected. The more pertinent the categories are to the system development work being done, the more rapidly data collects in them, and the more powerful are the predicting generalizations based on the data.

As we noted in the previous chapter, the tasks making up a job are defined along two dimensions:

1. The functions performed by the product of the job.
2. The activities performed to do the job.

To a large degree, the functions performed by a system varies with the system. Most systems incorporate the general functions of validating input data, updating records on the basis of the input data, data manipulating in the form of calculations and data rearrangements based on logical decisions, and producing reports. However, beyond this point, which doesn't take us far, significant variability occurs. Thus, task definition, from a functions point of view, is an area in which the project leader must depend on his knowledge of the system being developed. The metrics group, in turn, must depend on the project leader's knowledge in this area.

However, when it comes to the activities performed to develop a data processing system, standardization is possible. A given project may involve activities unique to it, although most activities on most projects are standard. You recognize the pattern as you move from one project to the next.

But unfortunately, at least at present, it's impossible to develop a list of standard system development activities across the data processing industry, because different installations develop systems differently and the complement of standard system development activities varies with the system development approach used. In these circumstances, the best an installation can do is develop a *standard system development activity list* for itself.

Even if an installation has no intention of developing time estimating standards or even collecting a time usage database, developing a standard system development activity list is worthwhile. If your installation shows no interest in developing such a list, develop one for yourself. The reason is as follows.

No matter how rough your time estimating techniques, they won't introduce as much error in your project plan as leaving tasks out of your project task list, since the estimated time to complete a task omitted from the task list is zero. From the point of view of adequate project planning, developing a complete task list is more important than developing precise time estimates for each task in the list.

When you're listing system functions to be taken into consideration when developing your project task list, you've little more to depend on than your knowledge of the system being developed. However, when listing the activities that have to be performed to complete your project, a standard system development activity list is an aid to ensure that activities aren't overlooked when the project task list is developed. For any given project, all the activities on the standard activity list may not be pertinent. But by methodically reviewing the standard activity list as you develop your task list, you guarantee that all activities, both pertinent to your project and on the standard activity list, are taken into consideration.

When developing a standard activity list, you can also develop the *standard dependencies* between the activities on the list. These standard dependencies can then be used as a check to ensure that you don't overlook any activity related dependencies when developing your bubble chart (in the same way a standard activity list can be used to ensure that you don't overlook any standard activities when developing your project task list).

5.1.2.3.2 Types of Standards.
If you're interested in establishing a metrics group and you use a structured methodology for system development, then DeMarco (1982) tells you how to do it. DeMarco even gives tentative standards for estimating. But he warns that the standards he supplies won't be much good. He doesn't believe, at least at the moment, that industry-wide standards are possible. His advice is to develop your own standards for your installation.

If your installation won't or can't afford to invest in a metrics group, then you're left to rely on rules of thumb for estimating, two types of which are:

1. *Ratios.*
2. *Algorithms.*

5.1.2.3.2.1 Ratios.
A ratio describes the relationship between the time required to do one task and the time required to do another. One such ratio says that it takes as long to *test a program*—develop the unit test plan, test data, and predetermined results; prepare the unit test operating instructions; and do the unit test—as it does to *prepare the program*—write the program specifications,

structure the program, and write the code. Such a ratio can be used in several ways:

1. If you've estimated the time required to prepare a program, you can also use it as an estimate of the time required to test the program.
2. If you've estimated the time required to prepare and test a program, half of this estimate is a good estimate of the time required to prepare the program.
3. If you've estimated the time required to prepare a program as being equal to the time required to test the program and you overrun your program preparation estimate, adjust your plans to anticipate a comparable program test overrun.

Another example says that the ratio between program development time and link test development time is eight to one. That is, if you estimate that it's going to take 40 person-months to develop the programs in a system, then plan on another five person-months to develop the link test for the system.

5.1.2.3.2.2 Algorithms. The following is an example algorithm for estimating the time to develop a program. It's a simplified version of an algorithm published by IBM in its *Management Planning Guide For A Manual Of Data Processing Standards*. The algorithm assumes that the program is to be written in COBOL or some other comparable language.

As already pointed out, the time needed to do a task is a function of the complexity of the task and the capabilities of the person assigned to the task. Thus, if we want to develop an algorithm to estimate program development time, we want to develop techniques for

1. Measuring program complexity.
2. Measuring a programmer's capabilities.
3. Combining these two measures into an estimate.

5.1.2.3.2.2.1 Program Complexity. DeMarco (1982, p. 122) identifies three dimensions of program complexity:

1. *Volume*—How big is the program?
2. Complexity itself, which we talk more about below.
3. *Adaptability*—How much of the code can be adapted from other sources— from previous work, from code libraries, or from toolkits such as a programmer's workbench?

DeMarco (1982, p. 120) defines complexity as the number of *decisions* in the program. The number of decisions is a dimension of complexity; however, we're not sure it gives adequate weight to the complexity involved in such program functions as *calculations* and *data rearrangements*. Consequently, we're driven back to the more subjective measure of complexity expressed by Bill Curtis, as quoted in DeMarco's book (1982, p. 118).

Complexity is a not-so-warm feeling in the tummy.

The algorithm combines volume and complexity by asking you to look at the functions of the program.

1. How many *inputs* does it have?
2. How many *outputs* does it have?
3. How much data rearrangement is involved?
4. How much decision making is involved?
5. How much calculation is involved?

Weights are assigned to inputs and outputs by counting them. Thus, if a program has two inputs and three outputs, its input output weight is five.

Weights are assigned to the data rearrangement, decision, and calculation functions by using the following table.

Function	Weight		
	Simple	Complex	Very Complex
Data Rearrangement	1	3	4
Decisions	1	4	7
Calculation	1	3	5

To use this table, you do two things for each function listed. First, you decide if the program involves the function. If it doesn't, you assign the function a weight of zero. If it does, you use the feeling in your tummy to decide where, on the continuum from simple to very complex, the complexity of the function lies. The weights in the table are guides, and you can interpolate. Thus, if you think the calculation function of a program is between simple and complex, you can assign it a weight of two.

As weighted in this table, complexity has two dimensions, *quality* and *quantity*. For example, if a program has a complex decision structure, the feeling in your tummy should move you up the decision complexity scale. On the other hand, none of the decisions in a program may be complex when taken by themselves, although there may be a lot of them. The quantity of decisions should also cause your tummy to move you up the decision complexity scale.

The measure of a program's complexity is the total weight assigned to it.

Thus, if our program with an input output weight of five were given a weight of one for data rearrangement, a weight of seven for decisions, and a weight of three for calculation, then the measure of the program's complexity is the total of the weights assigned, or 16.

DeMarco (1982, p. 122) tells us that the University of Maryland's Software Engineering Laboratory discounts the weight of adapted code to about 20% of the value which would otherwise be assigned. We use this adaptability factor as exemplified below.

Suppose we estimate that we'll adapt 10% of the code for the program which we previously weighted 16 for complexity; then 90% of this weight (0.9 × 16 = 14.4) won't change. The remainder (16 − 14.4 = 1.6) should be reduced to 20% of its original value, which is 0.2(1.6), or 0.32. Adding 14.4 and 0.32 gives an adjusted weight of 15.

5.1.2.3.2.2.2 Programmer Capability.   The algorithm measures the capabilities of the programmer assigned to the program on the basis of three dimensions:

1. How good a programmer is he in general?
2. How well does the programmer understand the application addressed by the system of which the program is a part?
3. To what degree is *application knowledge* (dimension 2 above) required to develop the program?

General programming skills involve

1. General knowledge of program development.
2. Familiarity with the language in which the program is to be written.

You categorize the programmer with respect to his general programming skills as senior, junior, or somewhere in between. A senior programmer is assigned a weight of 0.75, a junior programmer a weight of 3, and those in between 1.5. If appropriate, interpolate between these values.

The weight to be assigned to the combination of application knowledge possessed and application knowledge required is selected from the following table.

	Needed	
Possessed	Much	Some
A lot	0.75	0.25
Average	1.25	0.5
Some	1.5	0.75
None	1.75	1.0

Thus, the measure of the programmer's capability is the sum of the weights assigned to his general programming skills and the combination of application knowledge possessed and needed. Thus, a senior programmer with average applications knowledge, assigned to a program requiring some such knowledge, is given a weight of 0.75 plus 0.5, or 1.25.

5.1.2.3.2.2.3 Combining the Weights. The weight assigned to program complexity is multiplied by the weight assigned to programmer capability to give an actual time estimate. Thus, for our example program, the time estimate is 15 multiplied by 1.25, or 19 person days.

5.1.3 General Observations

When you estimate task time, your estimates aren't used solely to determine a schedule and make a cost estimate; task time estimates also set goals for people to meet. As C. Northcote Parkinson has observed, where people are concerned, work expands to fill the time allocated to it. Perhaps "at least" should be added. The point is that, if you make an estimate that's only slightly overrun, don't loosen up your estimating technique. Your estimate wasn't too tight, and the possibility exists that it's still too loose.

Another good general piece of advice is that, when possible, *estimate by committee*. Given the unreliability of our estimating techniques, getting several people to independently develop estimates isn't a bad idea. If the independently developed estimates tend to agree, maybe some enhancement in credibility for the estimate can be assumed. If the estimates don't agree, the estimators must be looking at different things. A conference, to determine what one person sees and another has overlooked or what one person sees that really isn't there, may result in a convergence toward a common estimate. The convergence must result from an agreement that estimating errors have been made; it must not result from negotiation. One source from which to get an independent estimate of the time required to complete a task is the person assigned to the task.

5.1.4 Summary

This is as far as we're going to wade into the murk. What can we say about what we've learned?

1. The best approach to estimating time is to develop standards. The only way to develop standards is to establish an independent metrics group that carries out the functions described by DeMarco (1982).
2. If your installation is unwilling to foot the expense of a metrics group or doesn't subscribe to the idea, and we believe most installations fall into this

category, then you're reduced to using rules of thumb—ratios and algorithms. We gave some examples of these rules of thumb in the section of this chapter on types of standards. Use them. And develop others, either by yourself or with your colleagues. Any methodical approach is better than none, because it opens the door to the possibility of detecting faults in the method. As this fault detection occurs, refine your methods accordingly.

3. Do the best time estimating job you can. But developing a complete task list and identifying all task dependencies and external restraints are more important than precise time estimates. DeMarco (1982) begins his book with the italicized slogan:

You can't control what you can't measure.

Not a bad slogan. But don't let it overwhelm you. It doesn't mean that, if you can't estimate task time precisely, you can't control your project. A complete list of detailed tasks and a complete identification of task dependencies and external restraints are more a measure of the dimensions of your project than most project leaders develop. Even with only rough rules of thumb for task time estimating, knowledge of the tasks making up your project and their dependencies, and knowledge of the external restraints within which your project must operate, gives you considerable control over your project.

4. Even with gross estimating techniques, the cause for severe system development overrun is seldom poor task time estimating; the more likely cause is poor project management. This book is concerned exclusively with project management. Yet only one section of one chapter of this book is devoted to task time estimating. If you experience a large overrun, it's unlikely that you'll be able to trace your problems back to faulty time estimating techniques. It is more likely that
   a. You didn't get a firm user identification.
   b. You didn't develop an adequate set of functional specifications.
   c. You didn't get design review committee approval of your design specifications before starting construction.
   d. You didn't enforce a request for change procedure.
   e. You didn't get agreement from the user on what constitutes system acceptance before entering acceptance testing.
   f. You overlooked necessary tasks.
   g. You overlooked task dependencies.
   h. You didn't get clearance for the delivery dates and turnaround rates on which you based your plans.
   i. You overburdened yourself with detailed tasks.
   j. You made inadequate allowance in your plans for contingencies.

k. You didn't use checkpoints to monitor progress.
l. You didn't control team member performance.
m. You allowed communications between you and either your user or your management to break down.

Inability to estimate precisely is a handy rationalization for ineffective management.

5.1.5 Example

In Appendix D are given the program specifications for one of the programs in the payroll system described in Appendix B. In Appendix E, we develop a time estimate to develop this program.

5.2 SITUATIONAL PLANNING

We've now come far in describing techniques for planning. We've talked about how to develop a task list, how to determine the dependency between tasks, how to identify external restraints, and how to estimate task time. In each case, we've described these techniques as if they should always be applied full-force. Such isn't the case.

When you're planning the construction phase of your project, intensive use of the planning tools we've described is appropriate. But when you're developing plans to project a target date and estimated project costs, and you have not yet done design or have not yet done either design or functional specification, the fineness with which you can apply planning tools diminishes. If you've just initiated a project and a plan is needed for an initial cost benefit analysis, your ability to develop a complete, detailed task list for the project and, consequently, your ability to develop a reliable plan are compromised. Do the best you can, but don't raise false expectations on your or anyone else's part. Your plan will necessarily be rough; so don't introduce specious detail. If you do, you're wasting time. And don't let anyone attach unjustified reliability to the target and cost estimates based on your plan. They can't be any more refined than the plan on which they're based and, consequently, incorporate a large standard deviation, the metric statisticians use to quantify expected variation about a point estimate.

We're teaching you planning skills. To use a skill properly, you must be adept at it; so know how to use these skills full-force. But being adept at a skill is only one part of using the skill properly. You must also exercise judgment with respect to the degree the skill is used in varying situations. When you're down to the short strokes, you use precision instruments. When you're on the tee, you use a blunter version of the same instrument that gives less precision but more distance for the same effort. As you move from one extreme to the other, you adjust the precision of your tools accordingly.

5.3 ASSIGNING PERSONNEL

Some rules of thumb for assigning personnel to tasks are

1. There must be some congruence between the demands of the task and the skills of the person assigned. Assigning a person to a task that underutilizes his skills has as many unfortunate consequences as assigning him to a task which is beyond his abilities. In the second case, you'll cause the person to fail and be responsible for any traumatic effects of the failure. In the first case, you'll cause the person to look for a job that will use his abilities. He may look outside the organization, which means you'll be responsible for losing him to another organization.
2. Within the limits in (1) above, assign a person tasks that give him an opportunity to increase both the range and depth of his skills.
3. Assign a person related tasks. Two benefits accrue:
   a. The work is more meaningful to the person. He sees his work as more of an interrelated whole rather than as a series of unrelated tasks.
   b. What the person learns in completing one task can be used to complete the other tasks more effectively.

   An example is to assign the task of unit testing a program to the person who wrote the program.
4. Certain tasks are more critical than others. For example, in the payroll system in Appendix B, the system is handicapped if program 5 won't run. But it's inoperable if program 1, 2, or 8 is down. It's also true that certain people are more reliable than others. Assign the more reliable people to the more critical tasks. The more reliable people aren't necessarily the more brilliant. A reliable person will work diligently on his assigned tasks and turn out reliable work in a reasonable time frame. In this regard, view an experienced new hire with caution. All you know about him is his resume. He may live up to it, in which case, all's well. But until his ability is demonstrated, exercise restraint in setting up circumstances where failure on his part puts you in an unrecoverable situation.

One aspect of task assignment is the question of what tasks you assign yourself. In making this assignment, take into consideration the fact that, by virtue of being project leader, you've assumed responsibilities which make demands on your time in proportion to the size of your project. If your project requires the concurrent assignment of more than five or six people, your time will be consumed by your project leader responsibilities.

For projects of smaller size, you can assign yourself tasks that consume some of your time. You're the project coordinator. Consequently, assign yourself tasks that keep you oriented to the system, rather than making you an expert on some part of the system. Therefore, writing the user manual and developing the link test are examples of the type of tasks to assign yourself.

Most projects are small enough to make you a first-line supervisor. That is, you're the first line of supervision in your organization. As a consequence, like other first-line supervisors, you must have an appreciation of the skills your people use, because when they run into trouble (that is, when they reach the limit of their skill level), it's to you that they'll look for help. They'll expect you to either provide help or know where to find it. This raises a question.

To perform this first-line supervisor function of skills enhancement, you're going to have to maintain your functional specification, design, and programming skills at a high enough level to perform this function. This doesn't mean you have to be the greatest analyst, designer and programmer who ever lived. It does mean you must keep current in these areas, so you can understand the team members when they explain their problems to you. How do you maintain this skill level if you never assign yourself a detailed task?

The answer is that, if you've assigned people according to the principle that their tasks require them to expand their skills, it will frequently be the case that a project member will encounter difficulty in completing his task and will come to you for help. Providing this assistance gives you the opportunity to remain in contact with the skills being used by the project members. The point isn't that you shouldn't get involved in detail—to the contrary, you should. The point is that you shouldn't tie yourself down to a specific detailed task. Instead, keep yourself flexible, so you can work on detail with the project member who needs help today. As soon as you've helped him, the chances are some other project member will then have developed a problem, and you should be free to move over and assist him.

Keeping yourself available for consultation identifies another characteristic of the tasks to assign yourself. These tasks should not be on the immediate *critical path*. Thus, if other demands prevent you from applying yourself to these tasks for days at a time, you aren't delaying overall project progress. Such tasks as writing the user manual and developing the link test also exhibit this characteristic.

PLANNING: PUTTING THE PLAN TOGETHER

6.1 DEVELOPING THE BAR CHART

If you follow the planning steps described in the previous two chapters, you now have the following planning information:

1. A bubble chart showing
   a. The tasks making up the job.
   b. The dependency between these tasks.
   c. The delivery dates on which these tasks depend.
2. A list of
   a. Deadlines.
   b. Turnaround rates.
3. Some idea of how personnel are going to be assigned to the tasks.
4. Some idea of how long it will take to do each task.

It's now time to combine this information into a task plan. A tool for organizing your planning information into a task plan is a *bar chart*.

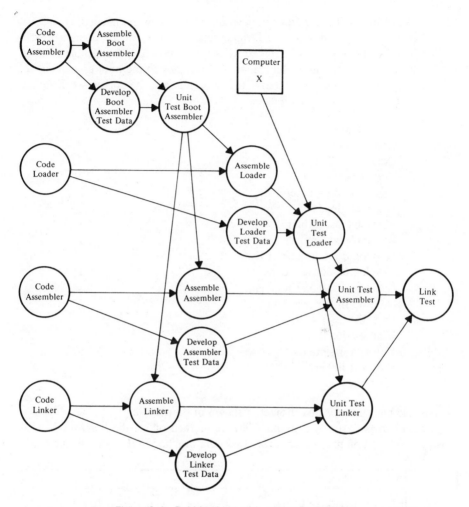

Figure 6-1. Bubble chart with external restraints.

6.1.1 The Bar Chart

Suppose we've developed the following information on our software system construction project:

1. Figure 6-1 is a bubble chart showing tasks, task dependency, and delivery dates.
2. The deadline for the software system is 30 weeks from now.
3. Computer X will first be available for testing purposes 17 weeks from now.
4. Unit test computer turnaround time is essentially instantaneous.

5. Blocks of link test computer time can be scheduled when needed.
6. Abbott, Baker, Chisholm, and Delaney are available for assignment to the project. Tentatively, we've decided to assign Abbott to the assembler, Baker to the linker, Chisholm to the loader, and Delaney to the boot assembler.
7. On the basis of the above tentative task assignments, the person-weeks to do each task are estimated as follows.

Code boot assembler	8
Code loader	3
Code assembler	12
Code linker	12
Assemble boot assembler	1
Assemble loader	1
Assemble assembler	1
Assemble linker	1
Develop boot assembler test data	2
Develop loader test data	1
Develop assembler test data	3
Develop linker test data	3
Unit test boot assembler	5
Unit test loader	1
Unit test assembler	8
Unit test linker	8
Link test	7

A possible bar chart for this project is shown in Figure 6-2.

A bar chart is basically a graph. Time is marked off on the horizontal axis. People are listed on the vertical axis. Tasks are graphed in the body of the chart

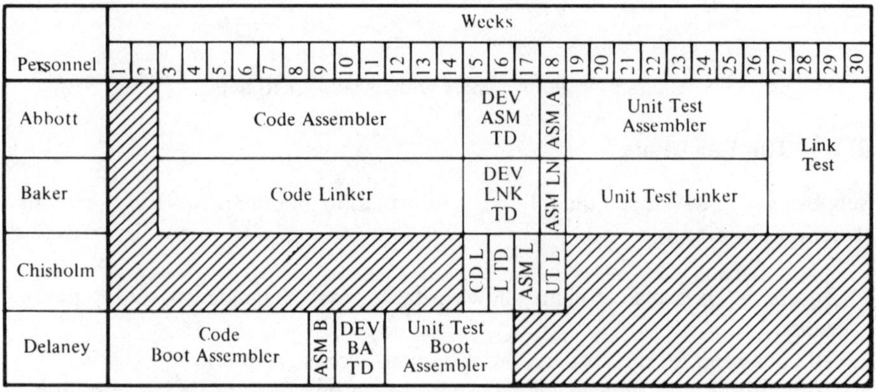

Personnel	Weeks (1–30)			
Abbott	Code Assembler	DEV ASM TD	ASM A	Unit Test Assembler
Baker	Code Linker	DEV LNK TD	ASM LN	Unit Test Linker
Chisholm		CD L / L TD / ASM L / UT L		
Delaney	Code Boot Assembler	ASM B / DEV BA TD	Unit Test Boot Assembler	

(Link Test appears at the right for Abbott and Baker.)

Figure 6-2. Bar chart.

to show who's going to do what task, when they're going to start, and how long it's going to take them.

The bar chart in Figure 6-2 was constructed as follows:

1. The two main parts of the system are the assembler and linker. Abbott has tentatively been assigned to the assembler and Baker to the linker. We decided that these two people should conduct the link test. Since this task requires seven person-weeks, and we're assigning two people to the task, we decided to set elapsed time at four calendar-weeks to allow for intra-task communication.

2. According to the bubble chart, both the assembler and linker are immediate predecessors of the link test. Since Abbott is going to be assigned to the assembler and Baker to the linker, and since both are to do the link test, there's no point in starting the link test until development of the assembler and linker is complete. The bar chart shows that we've scheduled link testing to begin in week 27. Therefore, the latest unit testing of the assembler and linker can be completed in week 26.

3. To use personnel most effectively, it was decided that one person would do all tasks related to developing a program. Consequently, Abbott was assigned all tasks related to developing the assembler, and Baker all tasks related to developing the linker. These tasks were arranged in the order—code, develop test data, assemble, and unit test for the following reasons:
   a. According to the bubble chart, coding must come before assembling or developing test data, and both of these latter two tasks must come before unit testing.
   b. Developing test data has no other dependencies, so it was scheduled before assembling, which is also dependent on the boot assembler being unit tested.

4. The bubble chart indicates that the loader must be unit tested before the assembler or linker can be unit tested. The bar chart shows that unit testing of the assembler and linker is to begin in week 19. Therefore, the latest the loader can be unit tested is week 18. Chisholm is assigned to this task. The other tasks involved in developing the loader are also assigned to him and were scheduled the same way as the assembler and linker tasks were scheduled for Abbott and Baker.

5. According to the bubble chart, before the loader, assembler, or linker can be assembled, the boot assembler must be unit tested. The bar chart shows that the loader is to be assembled before the assembler and linker and that the loader is to be assembled during week 17. Therefore, boot assembler unit testing must be complete at the end of week 16. This established the end point for the scheduling of the boot assembler development tasks, which were assigned to Delaney.

The method used for developing the bar chart in Figure 6-2 is called *backend loading*. A bar chart developed by this method has the following two features:

1. It's a task plan that schedules a job to be done in a minimum amount of time. To use PERT/CPM terminology, it establishes job time as critical path time. You can read the critical path off such a bar chart. For the bar chart in Figure 6-2, the critical path is all the boot assembler development tasks, the assembling and unit testing of the loader, the unit testing of either the assembler or the linker, and link testing. It could be maintained that assembling the boot assembler isn't on the critical path, since according to the bubble chart, it can be done in parallel with the development of the boot assembler test data. But it's impractical to assign these tasks to different people. As a consequence, both must be assigned to one person, which means they can't be done in parallel.
2. A backend loaded bar chart shows the *slack* available. Slack is another PERT/CPM term and can be defined as follows. If everybody starts working as soon as possible (week 1 in our case), slack is the time tasks can slip without postponing the completion date for the job. For example, in the bar chart in Figure 6-2, Abbott and Baker each potentially have two weeks of slack, Chisholm 14 weeks, and Delaney none. Backend loading squeezes all slack out of the schedule. Personnel aren't brought on the job until they must do their tasks on schedule to avoid having the job miss its deadline.

6.1.2 The Effect Of The Deadline

Being a textbook example, the task dependencies and delivery dates in our software development project mesh perfectly to allow all tasks to be done just in time to meet the deadline. However, if the deadline had been any tighter, it may be impossible to bring in the project on time. Thirty weeks is the minimum time in which the job can be done, unless some dependencies in the bubble chart can be relaxed.

For example, suppose the deadline is 29 weeks rather than 30 weeks. We said the dependencies in a bubble chart don't require a task's immediate predecessors to be complete before the task can be started, but do require that the immediate predecessors be complete before the task can be completed. Thus, in this situation, we could start looking for ways to overlap tasks and their immediate predecessors. For example, we might try to start assembling the loader before unit test of the boot assembler is complete. And we might try to start unit testing the assembler and linker before unit test of the loader is complete. In this way, we might save a week.

Such overlap of tasks and their immediate predecessors is sometimes possible. However, in the case of our software project, such planning is dangerous and must be avoided, because the chance that the overlap won't be realized is too high.

6.1.3 The Effect of Delivery Dates

The importance of delivery dates can't be overlooked either. For example, if computer X was first available 18 weeks from now, backend loading produces the bar chart shown in Figure 6-3. Here the deadline must be relaxed one week if the project is to remain possible. (The difference between the charts in Figures 6-2 and 6-3 is that, in Figure 6-2, the loader can be unit tested in week 18, while in Figure 6-3, it can't be unit tested until week 19.)

6.1.4 Rearranging Tasks

The bar chart in Figure 6-3 indicates that there's little overlap between Chisholm's and Delaney's schedules. If completion of the loader can be delayed one week, and if Chisholm has the skills to develop the boot assembler in the same time as Delaney, then Chisholm could take on responsibility for the boot assembler, and Delaney could be released for other assignments. This reassignment has two advantages and one disadvantage. The advantages are

1. Chisholm's work on the boot assembler will give him knowledge he can apply in developing the loader.
2. There are three, rather than four, people who have to communicate with each other. This will reduce intra-project communication time.

The disadvantage is that backup is reduced, so personnel loss carries a greater potential impact.

Personnel	Weeks (1–31)			
Abbott	Code Assembler	DEV ASM TD / ASM A	Unit Test Assembler	Link Test
Baker	Code Linker	DEV LNK TD / ASM LN	Unit Test Linker	
Chisholm		CD L / L TD / ASM L / UT L		
Delaney	Code Boot Assembler	ASM B / DEV BA TD	Unit Test Boot Assembler	

Figure 6-3. Bar chart in which a delivery date results in a later completion date.

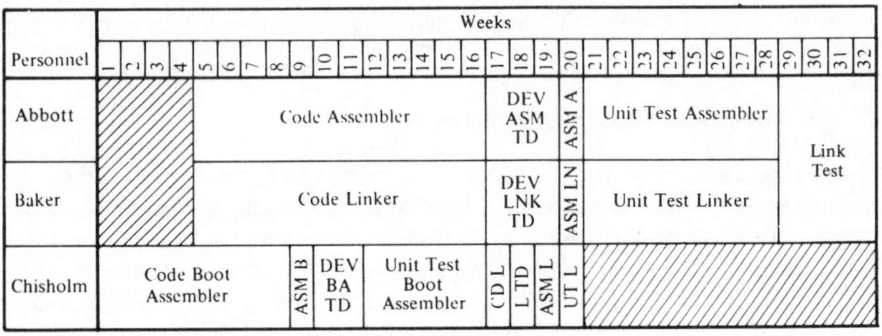

Figure 6-4. Bar chart with a relaxed project deadline.

However, these advantages and disadvantages are academic unless it's possible to delay the project completion date by one more week. This is because of the dependency between tasks. If unit testing of the loader is delayed one week, then unit testing of the assembler and linker is delayed one week, which delays link testing one week. A bar chart with this relaxed project deadline is shown in Figure 6-4.

Rearrangement of tasks in a bar chart is a normal operation in plan development. During this rearrangement, keep your bubble chart available for ready reference so, when rearranging, you don't inadvertently violate task dependencies.

6.1.5 The Effect Of Turnaround Rates

Let's see what happens to our bar chart if unit test computer turnaround deteriorates to the point where a person can productively spend only half of each day on assembly and unit test tasks. A backend loaded bar chart for this kind of external restraint is shown in Figure 6-5.

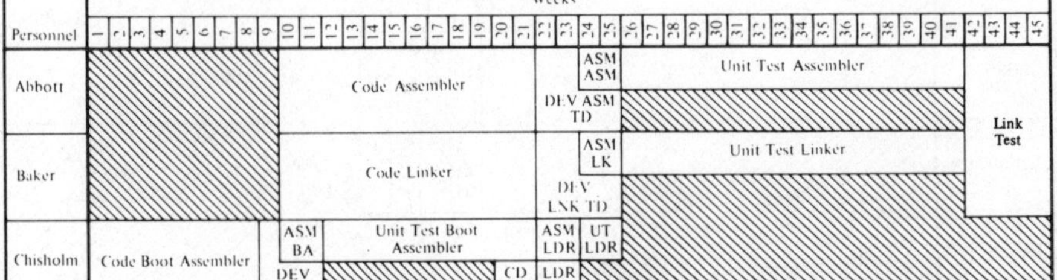

Figure 6-5. Bar chart with a reduced unit test computer time turnaround.

When we divided the link test task between Abbott and Baker, we saw the distinction between actual and elapsed time in one form. In Figure 6-5 we see the distinction in another form. For example, it still takes Abbott about eight person-weeks to unit test the assembler. But now these eight person-weeks are spread over at least 16 elapsed weeks. To be realistic, we should give Abbott more than 16 weeks to unit test the assembler. This would increase actual as well as elapsed task time. However, even without this refinement, we see the results of such a situation:

1. People are assigned multiple tasks to work on in parallel. For example, Baker is expected to finish developing the linker test data at the same time as he's assembling the linker.
2. People are required to work on multiple projects. For example, for most of the period during which Chisholm is unit testing the boot assembler, he's able to devote only half his time to the software project.
3. The completion date is delayed, because it's elapsed time, not actual time, that's meaningful as far as the critical path is concerned.

Incidently, it should never be necessary to assign a person more than two or, at most, three tasks, on the same or different projects, to be worked on in parallel. If this isn't the case, then working conditions at your installation are below the threshold necessary for maintaining motivated personnel. The people will be too disoriented to work productively and will, as a consequence, become demotivated.

Now that we have the plan shown in figure 6-5, the possibility of overlap of tasks and their immediate predecessors is increased. Specifically, since Abbott and Baker are performing only half-time unit testing, we could plan on starting the link test before unit testing the assembler and linker is complete, and thus, cut a week off the project length, as shown in Figue 6-6. Anticipating any greater overlap isn't realistic.

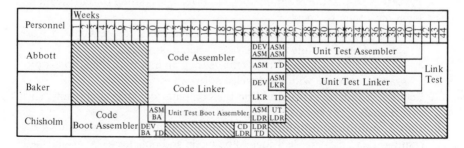

Figure 6-6. Overlapping tasks and immediate predecessors.

6.2 ALLOWING FOR CONTINGENCIES

A task is a schedulable activity. For example, unit testing the linker is a task. Thus, if we adopt Figure 6-4 as the bar chart for our software project, we can say that Baker will start unit testing the linker on week 21 and will work on this task for eight weeks. We can talk about the activity in terms of a schedule. We may turn out to be wrong, but at least it makes sense to talk in terms of when a person is going to start a task and how long it will take him to complete the task.

However, people spend time on activities other than tasks. For example, in unit testing the linker, Baker may discover a bug in the boot assembler. He may spend two days modifying the linker to get around the bug in the boot assembler. This is a legitimate activity, but it's not schedulable. It makes no sense to say, "On Tuesday of week 25 Baker will find a bug in the boot assembler, and it will take him two days to modify the linker to work around the bug." We call such activities *contingencies*.

Characteristic contingencies are as follows:

1. Temporary duty—A person on your project is required to temporarily attend to some special assignment. An example is a person who's required to fix a previously undetected bug in a production program.
2. Inadequate personnel skill—The persons assigned to the project don't possess the skills required by the tasks to which they must be assigned.
3. Transfer—A person is moved off your project because he's needed on a higher priority project.
4. Late delivery—Resources don't arrive on the agreed upon delivery dates. Examples of resources are personnel, hardware, software, and blocks of computer time.
5. Turnaround failure—Response time for repetitive services deteriorates below the level assumed when the plan was developed. An example of such services is running unit tests on the computer.
6. Software failure—The project uses a program not developed by the project and discovers that the program doesn't perform according to specifications. Time must then be spent
   a. Modifying project programs to get around the software bugs so work can go forward while the software is being corrected.
   b. When the revised software is released, again modifying the project programs to operate with the revised software.
7. Equipment failure—This could be the computer or other equipment, such as terminals, peripherals, or communications lines.
8. Lack of information—Information required for further progress isn't forthcoming. Examples are decisions to be made and policies to be established.
9. Attrition—A person on your project leaves the organization.

10. Absence—Sickness or excused time.
11. Company meetings: These are non-project-oriented meetings that the project personnel are required to attend. Examples are meetings on organizational changes and briefings on new employee benefits.
12. Promotion—A person is moved off your project because he has been promoted.

Another way to define contingencies is by saying what they aren't. For example, holidays, vacations, and leaves of absence aren't contingencies, because they can be scheduled.

So much for defining contingencies. Now, how do you provide for them in your plans? Since they can't be scheduled and since they're statistical in nature (the most we can say about them is that there's some probability they'll occur), the best we can do is make some kind of percentage allowance for them. For example, the bar chart in Figure 6-4 calls for 76 person-weeks of effort to complete the job. If we decide that contingencies are going to occur at a level of 10%, then the way to allow for contingencies is to build another seven or eight person-weeks of time into the bar chart. Building this contingency allowance into the bar chart is shown in Figure 6-7.

You may think that just blocking out another four elapsed weeks at the end of a task plan is too gross a way to allow for contingency. Our feeling is that you don't know when contingency will occur. Trying to allow for it in more detail is just refinement that doesn't increase precision.

We've just seen how, given a level at which you expect contingencies to occur, you can build an allowance for them in your bar chart. The question now is, How do you determine the level at which you expect contingencies to occur?

The fact that we can ask this question indicates that circumstances vary from project to project and that the contingency level varies with the circumstances. Consequently, the answer to the question is that you must rely on your knowledge of the circumstances to determine the expected contingency level.

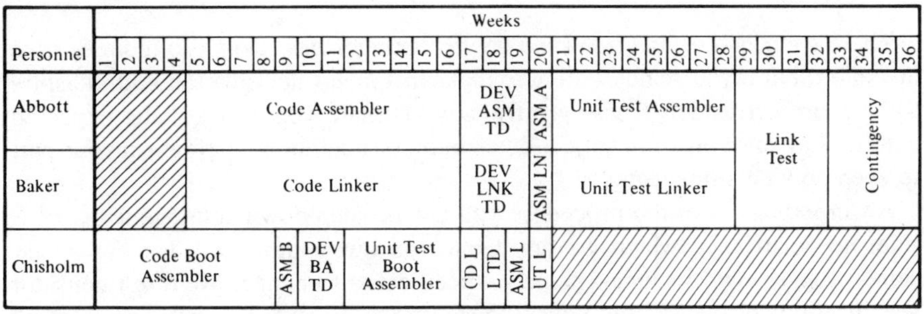

Figure 6-7. Contingency allowance.

However, there's a tool you can use to help evaluate the circumstances of your situation. This tool is a checklist of commonly experienced contingencies that you review item by item and ask yourself, To what extent do I expect·this type of contingency? The list of contingencies at the beginning of this section is a possible contingency checklist.

Typical questions you might ask when determining your expected contingency level are as follows:

1. Temporary duty—How recently have programs written by this programmer gone into production? How often do this person's programs break down in production? How volatile is the applications area in which his programs have been written? To what extent is this person called on to perform special assignments, such as making presentations or evaluating system designs?
2. Inadequate personnel skill and transfers—How deep is the department's bench? What's the probability that you'll be assigned regulars rather than recruits? What has been the recent history of personnel assignmens to projects in your department? How high is your project's priority?
3. Late delivery—What has been the delivery history of your supplier? Is your delivery to be one of the first production models?

Similar questions can be raised for the other types of contingencies on the checklist.

With respect to the range within which your expected contingency level might fall:

1. If your contingency experience remains at or below 10%, consider yourself a master project leader.
2. There's no upper limit to the extent to which contingency can occur. For example, if your assignment is to develop an application system with a computer or software system on which first delivery is yet to be made, an expected contingency level of 50% is conservative.

There's much you can do to keep down contingencies. Doing so requires time and effort, but if you're not willing to make this investment, you shouldn't aspire to be a project leader. Consequently, any estimate you make of the expected contingency level on your project takes into consideration an effort on your part to keep down contingencies.

As an indication of the procedure you use to keep down contingencies, consider an occurrence which we don't have on our contingency list but which some people would include—namely, specifications change. We don't consider specifications change a contingency because we do system construction under a request for change procedure whereby, if the functional specifications change, we can change our plans accordingly. As a consequence, we don't have to make allowance in our plans for specifications change. In other words, by anticipating the need for specifications change and providing for it, we eliminate it as a contingency.

To which you may reply, "Come off it, Gildersleeve. You're playing games. The fact that you adjust your plans for a specifications change doesn't alter the fact that the change introduces delay." We can't argue this point. But let us make several others:

1. The delay is tied to the specifications change, and the user must approve the delay.
2. Users don't like delays—delays foul up their plans.
3. Therefore, the user will avoid these delays. Specifically, he'll
   a. Avoid making frivolous requests for change.
   b. Apply himself to getting the specifications firmed up before construction so changes aren't necessary.

So while we can't deny that a request for change causes delays, the existence of the procedure reduces the number of requests.

Thus, the procedure for keeping down contingencies is to anticipate them and make provisions to minimize them. These provisions are as follows:

1. Make plans to avoid the contingency.
2. Clear your plans with the person who must perform if the contingency is to be avoided.
3. *Follow up* with this person to see that he performs.

Thus, the way to avoid contingencies is to convert them into external restraints.

For example, take temporary duty. If one of Abbott's production programs blows up, there's nothing you can do but grit your teeth and release him until he gets the problem straightened out. But if Abbott has a history of spending about 20% of his time on temporary duty, build this fact into your plan by showing on your bar chart that he's available for work on your project only four days out of five, and get your manager to approve your chart.

Again you can say, "But this doesn't eliminate the delay. It just recognizes the delay in the plan." To which we can only reply, "True." If a realistic plan shows an unacceptable completion date, adjustments must be made. Some of these adjustments must be made by your manager. Perhaps he can supply you with more person power or different people. Or perhaps something can be done to reduce Abbott's requirement for temporary duty. The point is that this approach requires you to both define your expectations and get commitments from resource suppliers to deliver according to your expectations. Only if delivery deviates from expectation will contingency occur. This approach minimizes the possibility of such deviation.

Inadequate personnel skill? Your plan must spell out the skill levels required. Get your manager to approve your plan. In doing so he's saying that, if you don't get the skills you need, you can't meet your deadline. Then if you don't get these skills, you can campaign for a relaxation of deadline.

This technique is known as covering your behind. The idea is: make clear what you need; get a commitment for delivery; follow up; and if delivery isn't made, put the blame where it belongs. But sticking someone else with the blame isn't the point. What's important is that, if you make your needs clear, get delivery commitments, and follow up, you minimize the probability that anything will go wrong in the first place.

Transfer? The approach is no different than the one for personnel skills—spell out in your plan the skill levels required and when they're needed, and have your manager approve your plan. If he assigns personnel to your project according to plan and subsequently transfers a person to another project, he does so only because the other project has higher priority. A conscious part of his decision must be that, because of relative priorities, he has downgraded the skill level on your project, and consequently, must relax your deadline.

Again and again in this section we say: get your manager's approval of your plan. Your plan should be of interest to your manager. Exercise every tactful effort to make him conversant with it. If he won't even look at it, let alone approve it, you're dealing with more contingency than you should take on.

Late delivery? Find out what realistic delivery dates are and develop a plan that coordinates with these dates. And get commitments on delivery that allow you to carry out your plan.

Turnaround? Find out what a realistic turnaround is (not the nominal one, the real one), and get a commitment on it. Develop your plans to conform to this turnaround.

Software failure? Hardware failure? These are tougher. But they're not immune to your expectations. Both software and hardware failures are really people failures. The performance of a person can be upgraded if he understands your expectations.

Lack of information? Spell out to the people, who must supply the information, what you need to know and when you need to know it. Anticipate your needs so the people have adequate time to develop the information on schedule.

Attrition? Minimizing this contingency is mostly a matter of motivation, which we address later in this book. However, another consideration is as follows. The longer project duration, the greater the possibility of turnover. Consequently, on a long project, the turnover should be built-in to occur automatically and harmlessly. This is done by initially overstaffing the project with junior people. It's the job of the juniors to understudy the senior people, and then, when the project is shaken out and well underway, the senior people, who are the most likely to be dissatisfied with being stuck on a project during a long construction phase, can be removed, for more productive work elsewhere, and replaced by the juniors who have been preparing for this takeover. Such an arrangement also allows juniors to obtain valuable experience.

Absence? Again this is a matter of motivation.

Company meetings? There's little you can do here. But this is a stable contingency that shouldn't have much impact on you if you plan for it.

Promotion? This is the only contingency you should encourage. Imagine the call on resources you could command if your reputation was that people who work on your projects always get promoted.

6.3 EXAMPLE

In Appendix F, we complete the development of the plan for the payroll system project described in Appendix B.

PLANNING: PROJECTING SCHEDULES AND COSTS

You've now spent considerable time learning how to develop a plan. Now we're going to investigate the relationship between plans, schedules, and cost estimates.

7.1 SCHEDULES

In Figure 7-1 is a plan for constructing a software system consisting of a loader, assembler, and linker for the new computer X. Once we have such a plan, establishing a schedule is child's play. For example, if anyone is interested in using the boot assembler, a glance at our plan establishes that the earliest the boot assembler is available is week 17. Similarly, if anyone is interested in using the loader, assembler or linker before they're link tested, earliest use dates are week 21 for the loader and week 29 for the assembler and linker. The earliest the

Personnel	Weeks 1–9	10–16	17–19	20	21–28	29–32	33–36
Abbott	/////	Code Assembler	DEV ASM TD	ASM A	Unit Test Assembler	Link Test	Contingency
Baker	/////	Code Linker	DEV LNK TD	ASM LN	Unit Test Linker	Link Test	Contingency
Chisholm	Code Boot Assembler · ASM B · DEV BA TD · Unit Test Boot Assembler		CD L · L TD · ASM L · UT L	/////////			

Figure 7-1. Plan.

loader, assembler and linker are available as a linked system is week 33, and we're not making commitments to deliver such a system until week 37. The point is that, if you don't have a plan, you can't supply a schedule.

7.2 COSTS

You may not be required to develop cost estimates. If so, fine. Otherwise, here's how to do it.

We've already demonstrated that, if you don't have a plan, you can't supply a schedule. Similarly, without a plan, you can't supply a cost estimate either. While a schedule can be read directly from your plan, converting a plan into a cost estimate requires more work. A form to develop a cost estimate is shown in Figure 7-2. The form is used as follows.

7.2.1 Personnel

Salary is only a part of *personnel costs*. The remainder of personnel costs are the costs to supply such personnel support services as working space, furniture, filing facilities, stationery supplies, clerical support, reproduction facilities, employee benefits, management, and administration. These costs are called *overhead* and are generally factored into personnel costs as a percentage of salary. Usually, the *rate structure* used to extend person-weeks into dollars includes both salary and overhead. For example, if Abbott, Baker, and Chisholm are each paid $750 a week, and if (in the organization in which we're doing our software project) overhead is 100% of salary, then the applicable rate for a week of work by Abbott, Baker, or Chisholm is $750 for salary costs plus $750 for overhead costs, or $1500.

From the plan in Figure 7-1, we see that Abbott and Baker will each work 32 weeks on the project, and Chisholm will work 20 weeks. Extending these times

COST ESTIMATE

PROJECT NO.		PROJECT PHASE	
PREPARED BY			DATE

PERSONNEL

NAME	WEEKS	SALARY	COST
			TOTAL

COMPUTER TIME _____

TRAVEL AND LIVING EXPENSES _____

SUPPORT SERVICES	COST
	TOTAL

GRAND TOTAL

Figure 7-2. Cost estimate form.

by the rate structure of $1500 a week, we arrive at a personnel cost of $48,000 each for Abbott and Baker, and $30,000 for Chisholm, for a total personnel cost of $126,000, as shown in Figure 7-3.

The point we're developing here is that a cost estimate is a plan extended by a rate structure.

COST ESTIMATE

PROJECT NO. *12345*	PROJECT PHASE *Construction*	
PREPARED BY *Tom Gildersleeve*		DATE *8/1/84*

PERSONNEL

NAME	WEEKS	SALARY	COST
Abbott	*32*	*$1500*	*$48,000*
Baleer	*32*	*1500*	*48,000*
Chisholm	*20*	*1500*	*30,000*

TOTAL *$126,000*

COMPUTER TIME _____ *25,200*

TRAVEL AND LIVING EXPENSES _____ *—*

SUPPORT SERVICES	COST

TOTAL *—*

GRAND TOTAL *$151,200*

Figure 7-3. Cost estimate.

7.2.2 Computer Time

Although computer time typically isn't planned, *computer time costs* are sometimes included in a cost estimate. Computer time costs are projected as a percentage of personnel costs. This percentage is a function of both personnel costs and computer time costs and varies with both installation and the passage of time. Apply the percentage currently used at your installation. For example, if the percentage is 20, computer time cost for our software project is 20% of $126,000, or $25,200, as shown in Figure 7-3.

7.2.3 Travel And Living

A third category of cost is *travel and living,* which is sometimes built into over-head. However, if this cost isn't built-in and your project requires travel, it's a significant cost. With respect to travel and living, the rate structure is evident. You can get a quote on airline and car rental rates. Company policy dictates an allowance for automobile mileage. Even if actual living expenses are charged, per diem rates can be developed for locations to be visited. To arrive at a cost estimate for travel and living, it's necessary to develop a travel plan—who's going where, how often are they going, how long are they going to stay each trip, and are they going to have to rent a car? Once the travel plan is determined, developing the cost estimate is a matter of applying rates to the plan.

7.2.4 Support Services

A fourth category of cost is *support services.* In this category fall all the services a project might contract for with some outside supplier of services—another department of the organization or a vendor. Some examples of support services are consultant services, proprietary software, equipment, and publication of manuals.

The cost estimate for a support service is obtained from the supplier. The rate structure isn't always apparent, but the existence of one is apparent from the fact that a supplier won't provide you with a quotation until you tell him what service you want. The consultant wants to know what you expect him to do, the software house and equipment vendor want to know what configuration you want of the options offered, and the publisher wants to know how many copies of the manual you want and how many pages and illustrations there'll be in the manual. In other words, the supplier wants you to make a plan, then he applies his rate structure to the plan and arrives at a cost estimate with which he supplies you.

7.3 BUDGETS AND DEADLINES

Thus, for all categories of cost, developing a cost estimate is a matter of applying a rate structure to a plan. As a result, a cost estimate can't be reliable unless it's backed by a plan. Therefore, if you're presented with a budget, it's appro-priate to ask for the plan on which it's based. You must review the plan to see if you can follow it, for if you can't, the cost estimate may be unrealistic.

If you're presented with a budget either unsupported by a plan or supported by an unrealistic plan, this doesn't mean the budget is inadequate, but it does make it suspect. You must then consider the budget an external restraint and see if you can develop a plan that fits within the budget. If you can, you're on solid ground. If you can't, then you, your manager, and your user are in trouble, for decisions are being based on unrealistic cost estimates. You're obligated to make your manager aware of this fact.

The worst a project leader can do when given a job to be done with inadequate resources is to say, "I'll try." As Robert Townsend, in his book *Up The Organization,* quotes Napoleon:

> A commander in chief cannot take as an excuse for his mistakes in warfare an order given by his minister or his sovereign, when the person giving the order is absent from the field of operations and is imperfectly aware or wholly unaware of the latest state of affairs. It follows that any commander in chief who undertakes to carry out a plan which he considers defective is at fault; he must put forward his reasons, insist on the plan being changed, and finally tender his resignation rather than be the instrument of his army's downfall. (p. 35)

With the exception of the fact that Napoleon neglects to mention the possibility that the sovereign may be able to demonstrate the plan's soundness to the commander in chief, Napoleon's advice is to the point.

If you've been assigned a project with an unrealistic budget or deadline; are unable to convince those with the ability to do so to modify the project, budget or deadline; and don't want to take Napoleon's advice on resigning; then remember: when the money or time runs out, you're in a better position if you deliver an incomplete but operable system rather than if you can't show anything for your work, no matter how close to completion you are. For example, if the project is the payroll system described in appendix B, when the money or time

Personnel	1	2	3	4	5	6	7	8	9	10	11	12	13	14	15	16	17	18	19	20	21	22	23	24	25	26	27	28	29	30	31	32
																		Weeks														
Abbott	/////	/////	/////	/////	Code Assembler													DEV ASM TD		ASM A	Unit Test Assembler								Link Test			
Baker	/////	/////	/////	/////	Code Linker													DEV LNK TD		ASM LN	Unit Test Linker								Link Test			
Chisholm	Code Boot Assembler								ASM B	DEV BA TD		Unit Test Boot Assembler					CD L	LTD	ASM L	UT L	/////	/////	/////	/////	/////	/////	/////	/////	/////	/////	/////	/////

Figure 7-4. Plan with no contingency allowance.

runs out, you're better off having programs 1, 2, and 8 ready (even if you have not done another thing) rather than having the system 95% developed but non-operational.

Even if you believe the budget and deadline for your project are realistic, develop your plan to get up a minimal but operable system first, and then flesh out this nucleous system. You then have a fallback position if unanticipated contingencies overwhelm you.

7.4 CONTINGENCY ALLOWANCE

It's sometimes proposed that, instead of building a contingency allowance in your plan, it be built into the cost estimate only. For example, in Figure 7-4 there is a plan identical to the one in Figure 7-1 except that the plan in Figure 7-4 has no contingency allowance. Costing out the plan in Figure 7-4 yields a personnel cost of $114,000 and a computer time cost of $22,800, for a total of $136,800. If we expect contingency at a level of 10%, this total cost is boosted by 10% to $150,480, which is the quoted cost and includes a contingency allowance of $13,680.

The theory behind this kind of contingency allowance is that the schedule isn't to be allowed to slip, and if the project gets into difficulty, the dollars in the contingency allowance are to be used to buy additional resources to bail out the project. Possible resources purchased might be added personnel, additional computer time, or some support services.

However, because of other factors, such as unavailability of more computer time or lack of knowledge concerning the project on the part of new personnel, the convertibility of dollars into resources often turns out to be more sticky than promised. As a consequence, if you've a choice, build your contingency allowance into your plan.

7.5 EXAMPLE

In Appendix G, we develop a cost estimate for the plan developed in Appendix F.

DIRECTING ACTIVITIES

In this chapter we're concerned with your responsibilities with respect to the ongoing activities in which the project members engage in their collective effort to reach the project goal. We begin this investigation with an example that both summarizes the planning topics discussed in Chapters 4–7 and leads into the topic of directing activities.

8.1 THE USE OF PLANS

Suppose you're in New York and want to drive to Boston. The first thing you do is get a road map and decide what route to take. You might decide on the route as shown in Figure 8-1. Here you take Route 95 to New Haven, Route 91 to Hartford, Route 84 (which changes into Route 86) to Sturbridge, and Route 90 to Boston.

This route map is a plan for getting from New York to Boston. Two observations are appropriate.

1. Once you have your plan, you can quote a schedule—you can tell anyone who's interested when you'll arrive in New Haven, Hartford, Sturbridge, and Boston.

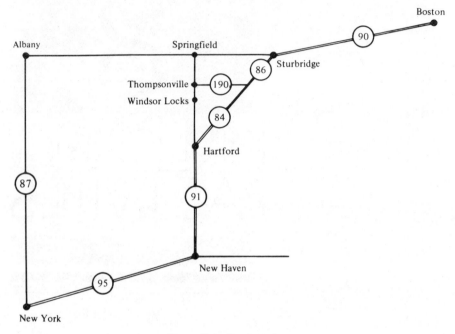

Figure 8-1. Route map.

2. You can also provide anyone who wants it with a cost estimate—you can measure off the miles on your route and extend this figure by the appropriate cents a mile rate.

However, you use your plan for a third purpose, also. You use it to direct your progress as you move from your origin to your destination. Reflect on the fact that, if you hadn't made your plan before you started, when you drove your car out of your driveway, you wouldn't know which way to turn!

Our analogy between a car trip and a project has one other moral, which is that planning isn't a one-time thing. As you progress toward your destination, progress begins to deviate from your plan. It then becomes necessary to modify your plan to maintain your best posture toward your goal.

For example, suppose it's an hour since you left New Haven, and you're still on Route 91—you have not found the exit to Route 84. All of a sudden, you see an exit marked "Windsor Locks," which strikes you as strange, so you pull over to the side and look at your map. Sure enough, Windsor Locks is north of Hartford—you've missed the exit to Route 84. Now you must decide what you're going to do—are you going to go back to Hartford and pick up Route 84, continue north on 91 until you hit Route 90, or go to Thompsonville and cut across Route 190 to get back on plan? Regardless of your decision, notice two things.

1. Without a plan, you can't tell whether you're on course or not.
2. Once you determine that you're off course, your plan provides the context in which you decide what you're going to do next.

Keep in mind when developing a plan that you aren't only developing a mechanism with which to project a schedule and estimate a cost, you're also developing the tool you use and modify to guide your project's progress toward its goal.

Finally, the schedule and cost estimate you project from your plan have meaning only if you follow your plan. For example, if instead of following the route outlined in Figure 8-1, you take Route 87 to Albany and Route 90 to Boston, any schedule and cost estimate based on the plan are meaningless.

Planning is one of the project leader's coordination responsibilities. The other two are monitoring progress and controlling performance.

8.2 DIRECTING ACTIVITIES

We analyze your responsibilities in directing activities into two areas.

1. Monitoring the schedule.
2. Controlling performance.

When you're monitoring a project member's schedule, you're trying to answer the question, "Is the project member on time?"

When you're controlling a project member's performance, you're trying to answer the question, "Is the project member doing what he's supposed to do?" Perhaps an example will clarify this question. Suppose you've assigned Kramer to develop program 8 in the payroll system in Appendix B. It's going to be weeks and perhaps months before any of program 8 is ready for unit test. In the meantime, the question that keeps rumbling around in the back of your mind is, "Is this program Kramer is writing going to do anything that program 8 is supposed to do?" This question epitomizes the problem of control.

The question of whether a project member is on time isn't independent of the question of control. For example, if at the end of nine weeks, Kramer tells you he has the code for program 8 completed, then presumably he's on time. However, if unit testing demonstrates that his code has logical problems and chunks of it have to be ripped out and replaced, then not only was Kramer's performance not controlled, but he didn't have the code done on time either.

Nevertheless, the tools you use to monitor a project member's schedule are different from the tools you use to control his performance. Consequently, we're going to analytically separate these two functions and discuss them one at a time. Thus, in this Chapter, we first concern ourselves with monitoring the schedule and then take up the topic of controlling performance.

8.2.1 Monitoring The Schedule

Let's represent the problem of monitoring a project member's schedule graphically, as shown in Figure 8-2. The horizontal axis of the graph in this figure represents time. The vertical axis represents the effort a person puts in during one day.

Suppose we have a task to be done, such as a program to be developed. Let's suppose we give this task to Charlie.

We mark on our graph when we expect Charlie to finish the task. The upright bar on the right of the graph in Figure 8-2 represents this deadline. Then the origin of our graph represents where we are today, and the baseline between the origin and the deadline represents the number of workdays we expect to pass before Charlie finishes.

We've marked with an arrowhead on the vertical axis of our graph the point that represents the effort we expect from Charlie in a normal workday.

Suppose we expect Charlie to start today and work full-time on his task to get finished in time to meet his deadline. Then the area under the horizontal line, across the top of our graph from the point of a normal workday's effort to Charlie's deadline, represents the effort we think Charlie has to expend to get his task done. Thus, if we've estimated well, Charlie should be able to put in a normal effort each workday and meet his deadline without difficulty.

But what does Charlie's effort curve really look like? If Charlie is typical, his effort curve looks like the one in Figure 8-3. As a result, Charlie may, in the early days of his task, dig himself such a hole that, even though, as his deadline nears, he puts in more and more effort, to the point where he's working considerable amounts of overtime on his own, he finds it impossible to recover and misses his deadline.

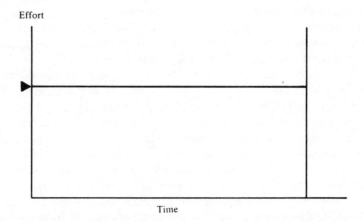

Figure 8-2. The amount of effort needed to do a task.

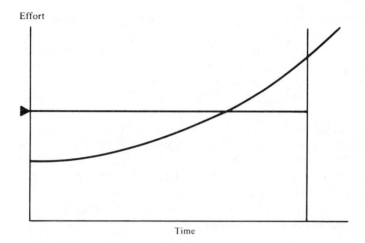

Figure 8-3. Typical effort curve.

So Charlie overran his deadline. This is the situation we want to avoid, and it's what monitoring the schedule is all about. But before we try to figure out what we can do to keep Charlie on schedule, let's first try to determine why he fell behind.

8.2.1.1 Why Deadlines Are Missed. The chances are low that Charlie was late because he's a malingerer. The fact that he put in so much extra effort toward the end of his task in an attempt to recover lost time argues against such a contention. No, the situation that led to Charlie's downfall is more prosaic.

At any given point in time, there are a number of activities contending for Charlie's attention. Not only is there the task we've given him, but there are other work related goals.

1. There are correspondence, brochures, and periodicals to read.
2. There are meetings, seminars and classes to attend.
3. There are things to discuss with fellow workers.
4. And there's research to do.

In addition to these work related goals, Charlie has personal goals contending for his attention.

1. He needs a haircut.
2. He has to buy his wife an anniversary present.
3. He has matters to iron out with his lawyer.
4. And this week's football pool hasn't been worked up yet.

To allocate his time among these goals, Charlie assigns them priorities. One of the dimensions on which Charlie ranks goals is the importance they take on in his eyes. Thus, he might consider getting his wife's present the most important thing he has to do. Doing his task might rank second. And so on.

However, another dimension on which Charlie ranks goals is the immediacy with which each goal can or must be achieved. As a result, although Charlie agrees that getting his task done is more important than reading brochures and working out the football pool, the fact that it only takes a few minutes a day to read the brochures and the fact that the football pool must be worked out before the end of the week causes him to assign a higher priority to reading brochures and working out the football pool than he assigns to getting his task done. As a consequence, Charlie continues to spend portions of his time pursuing short-term goals until his deadline begins to assume the proportions of a short-term goal. But by then it may be too late.

8.2.1.2 Checkpoints. If the pursuit of short-term goals is the reason why people miss deadlines, then the solution is to have short-term goals for a series of subtasks that make up the task, instead of having one long-term deadline. We call these short-term goals *checkpoints*.

It is likely that Charlie will behave toward checkpoints the same as he did toward his deadline. But when he misses a checkpoint, all is not lost—the deadline hasn't yet been breached, and there's still time to recover. Thus, checkpoints act as an early warning system to give you the opportunity to provide aid before a deadline is missed.

But more importantly, checkpoints act as a self-pacer device for the person doing the task. When he misses a checkpoint, he knows he's behind schedule and he can henceforth maintain a high level of effort until he gets back on schedule.

To perform their functions, checkpoints must have certain characteristics. First, as we've already said, checkpoints must be separated by short periods of time; otherwise, they aren't short-term goals. Checkpoints separated by less than a week are harassment rather than pacers. Ones separated by more than a few weeks (two, three, or four) lose their short-term characteristic. Checkpoints separated by a week or two are ideal. However, checkpoints can't be set up arbitrarily, as we will see in the second characteristic of a good checkpoint.

The second characteristic of a good checkpoint is that it must be easy to determine whether the checkpoint has been reached. This prevents differences of opinion between you and the project member on whether he has reached his checkpoint. But more importantly, it allows the project member to determine for himself whether he has reached his checkpoint.

To easily determine whether a checkpoint has been reached, the checkpoint must be tied to something that's both objective and part of the task. Examples of such things are the production of some product, such as program specifications, or the occurrence of some event, such as successful running of a test.

The third characteristic of a good checkpoint is that the person who must meet it must consider it realistic; otherwise, his failure to meet it won't tell him he's behind. For checkpoints to be realistic in a person's eyes, they must be his own, that is, a person must be the one who sets his checkpoints. We say more about establishing checkpoints in a later section of this chapter.

8.2.1.3 Measuring Progress.

When setting checkpoints, a project member subdivides his task into finer subtasks. As indicated by the requirement that each subtask be defined in terms of a deliverable end product, these subtasks are no different than the tasks you set up when developing your project plan; they just divide the plan into a finer set of tasks. This provides you with a detailed calibration for measuring *progress*. For example, if a job is divided into 50 tasks, when you measure the degree of job completion, you can talk about having ten, 15, or 27 tasks done. Another reason for separating checkpoints by short periods is that the more finely you divide a job into tasks, the more precisely you measure the degree of job completion.

8.2.1.4 Establishing Checkpoints.

For the project member who completes tasks on time, establishing checkpoints is no problem, because he must already be using them. If he's using them explicitly, all you have to do is ask him what they are. If he's using them implicitly, a little orientation should make him aware of what he's doing. At that point, he should, once more, be able to tell you what his checkpoints are. In any case, at all times, it must be clear to the project member that the only reason you're establishing checkpoints on his tasks is to measure project progress. There should be no implication that the checkpoints are being established because you question his ability to stay on schedule. Such a question is misplaced and demotivating.

For the project member who has trouble meeting deadlines, you've work to do. If checkpoints are going to help the project member stay on schedule, he must set them. But you can't let him do this unilaterally. The checkpoints must be reasonable to him, but they must be reasonable to you, also. Thus, the following approach is necessary.

First, you must decide what you think is a reasonable time for completing the task to which the person is assigned. This is no problem, since you did this when you developed your plan.

Next, you invite the project member to set his checkpoints. When you do, you don't tell him what your task time estimate is. Otherwise, rather than trying to estimate the time needed to complete each of the subtasks making up his task, he may just divide your task time among the subtasks. When the project member proposes his checkpoints, there are two possibilities.

1. The checkpoints appear reasonable. In this case, you accept them.
2. The checkpoints seem unreasonable. In this case, you do the following.

The project member's checkpoints look either too tight or too loose to you. In either case, he must have arrived at them from different assumptions than you used. Consequently, the first step is to ask him how he arrived at his checkpoints. If he can demonstrate that his reasoning is sound, then once more, accept his checkpoints. You must now modify your plans. This is unfortunate, but better now, when you can give warning of the change, than later, when people depending on your delivery no longer have the opportunity to modify their plans.

On the other hand, if you find the project member's reasoning deficient, there's a question you can ask. For example, if it appears he overlooked something, you can say, "And you've included the time to generate test data (or whatever the something is) in your estimate?" In so doing, you get him to arrive at acceptable checkpoints without suggesting what they should be. You now have a reasonable set of checkpoints that were established by the project member, not you. He should be encouraged to think of them as his.

Most project members set checkpoints too tightly. With such people, the above approach works. For the person who sets checkpoints you think are too loose, you have a bigger problem. In trying to arrive at a common set of assumptions from which agreeable checkpoints can be derived, you're in danger of revealing what you think a reasonable time estimate is. If you make this revelation, the project member may switch from time estimating to negotiation or regurgitation, which defeats the object of checkpoints. Before this happens, you're better off letting the project member stick with his checkpoints. If he persists in his estimates, you've no choice but to accept them. But you must then monitor him closely to determine that he's putting in full effort, rather than converting his checkpoints into self fulfilling prophesies.

8.2.1.5 Monitoring Checkpoints. After checkpoints have been set up, you must periodically (at least every week or two, preferably every week) check with your project members on their achievement in meeting checkpoints. You do this to monitor your project's progress against your plan. These follow-ups should be done strictly in terms of collecting data for project plan monitoring. Any other attitude will be seen by the project members as an indication of distrust, which is demotivating.

You concentrate on failure to meet checkpoints in the following situations only:

1. A project member asks for help in meeting checkpoints.
2. A project member consistently misses checkpoints.

In these situations, a *performance review,* to determine the difficulty and explore possible solutions, is appropriate. Performance reviews are discussed in the chapter on motivation.

8.2.1.6 Example. In Appendix H, we develop a checkpoint plan to monitor the progress of each project member as he works on the tasks assigned to him in the plan developed in Appendix F.

8.2.1.7 Meeting Checkpoints. In Appendix H, we set up checkpoints to monitor the progress of the project members working on the payroll system described in Appendix B. Now, what can we do to maximize the probability that the project members meet their checkpoints? Think about what your answer to this question is before reading on.

Chances are you didn't come up with a satisfactory answer. Let's try a different approach. List the reasons you've heard for missing checkpoints. Inspection of this list may give you a clue on how to improve the probability of meeting checkpoints. Draw up this list before reading on.

That was easier, wasn't it? A partial list of reasons given for missing checkpoints is shown below. Your list will be similar.

1. I had to fix a bug in one of my other programs.
2. It took two days to get back my test shot.
3. Charlie hasn't generated the information I need.
4. There's a bug in the data management system.

There's no point in continuing. What we're generating is a list of contingencies. It's contingencies that are cited as reasons for missing checkpoints.

Therefore, to maximize the probability of meeting checkpoints, keep down contingencies. When discussing planning, we emphasized the importance of this project leader function. The importance can now be more fully appreciated. Contingencies have a negative effect on performance at three levels:

1. Contingencies delay people.
2. Contingencies are demotivators. Suppose you sit down with Charlie and develop checkpoints for monitoring his schedule. You then let many contingencies occur that prevent him from meeting his checkpoints. What will happen the next time you try to set checkpoints with Charlie? If he's an introvert, he'll go through the exercise, but inwardly, he'll consider it futile. On the other hand if he's an extrovert, he'll laugh in your face. In either case, you've lost the motivation that checkpoints can provide.
3. Contingencies are used as excuses for failure. As Robert Townsend (1971, p. 41) puts it:

When you get right down to it, one of the most important tasks of a manager is to eliminate his people's excuses for failure. But if you're a paper manager, hiding in your office, they may not tell you about the problems only you can solve. So get out and ask them if there's anything you can do to help. Pretty soon they're standing right out there in the open with nobody but themselves to blame. Then they get to work, then they turn on to success, and then they have the strength of ten.

8.2.1.8 What To Do When Checkpoints Are Missed. Despite your best efforts, checkpoints will be missed. When a checkpoint is missed, there are several things you should do:

1. You should determine what caused the failure. This is important for two reasons:
   a. The cause may be general and make other project members miss their checkpoints, too.
   b. Even if the cause is peculiar to this individual, it may cause him to miss other checkpoints as well.
   Determining the cause is problem solving, which we can't get into in this book. But one thing of which you should be aware is that the reason a person gives for missing a checkpoint may not be the cause. For example, he may complain of poor data entry service when the cause may actually be poor handwriting. For more on problem solving, see the chapter "Creative Thinking" in *Successful Data Processing System Analysis.*
2. Once you determine the cause, take steps to eliminate it.
3. See that what has to be done to recover is done. Perhaps extra effort on the person's part will get him back on schedule. Perhaps he needs some help, either from you or from someone you can get temporarily assigned to such duty.
4. If the checkpoint has been missed badly and no recovery procedure available to you is going to prevent overrunning the deadline, you must tell those people, who're depending on delivery, of the slippage *immediately.* The sooner they're told, the more chance they have to adjust their plans.

8.2.2 Controlling Performance

So far in this book we've discussed planning and monitoring the schedule. In describing the techniques for performing these project leader functions, we've concentrated on their application to system construction. However, with the qualification of increasing fuzziness of the applicable task list, these techniques also apply to system design and functional specification.

We're now ready to address the question of controlling performance. The problem of controlling performance is the attempt to answer the question, "Is the team member doing what he's supposed to do?"

You want to control team member performance during functional specification and design as well as during construction. Yet the purpose of each of these activities is different. This leads to the idea that the method for controlling performance during each activity is different, and such is the case. As a consequence, when we address the subject of controlling performance, we must do it one activity at a time. We must discuss the techniques for controlling performance during functional specification, the techniques for controlling performance during design, and the techniques for controlling performance during construction.

We might get a better understanding of these varying control techniques if we've a clear understanding of what we're trying to do in each system development activity.

The purpose of construction is to build a system that conforms to the specifications laid down during functional specification and design.

The purpose of design is to decide how to construct the system so it will function as specified in the functional specifications. There's more than one way to construct the system so it functions as specified. These designs are considered better or worse in a variety of ways depending on point of view. The computer center considers the design from the point of view of how smoothly the specified system will fit into its operating environment. The maintenance group considers the design from the point of view of how easy the system is to maintain. The internal auditors consider the design from the point of view of how amenable the system is to audit. The quality assurance group considers the system from the point of view of how efficiently it uses available data processing facilities and how flexible it is. These points of view conflict. The purpose of design is to settle on a design that effects the optimum compromise between conflicting interests. Such a design is the best of the alternatives.

The purpose of functional specification is to come to an agreement with the user as to what the system is to do.

In summary, the purpose of the three system development activities are as follows:

1. Functional specification—Come to an agreement with the user as to what the system is to do.
2. Design—Determine the best design for the system.
3. Construction—Construct the system according to specifications.

Thus:

1. During functional specification you're looking for performance that results in agreement with the user as to what the system is to do.

2. During design, you're looking for performance that results in the best system design.
3. During construction, you're looking for performance that results in a system constructed according to specifications.

It's now time to turn our attention to the techniques you use to control performance during functional specification, design, and construction so the performance produces the results appropriate to the purpose of the activity.

8.2.2.1 Construction. What techniques should you use to control project member performance during construction so their performance produces a system constructed according to specifications?

8.2.2.1.1 Testing. Testing is the essential construction control technique.

8.2.2.1.1.1 Acceptance Testing. The ultimate test is the acceptance test.

8.2.2.1.1.2 Link Testing. But the term, acceptance test, is a misnomer. The acceptance test is a demonstration to the user that the system performs as specified. That such is the case, however, should first be proven through link testing.

8.2.2.1.1.3 Unit Testing. Prior to link testing comes unit testing. Study after study has demonstrated that effectiveness and efficiency of unit testing is independent of the tools used (Demarco, 1982, p. 217). Whether testing is online or batch, the critical element is good *test procedures.*

Unit testing should be organized. Each time the program is submitted to testing, the programmer should know what program functions are to be tested, and the test data should have been designed specifically to test these functions. The more effectively test data is developed, the more effective and efficient unit testing is.

After a test shot, the results are compared against predetermined results to see if the program performed correctly. If it did, the next test shot is performed to test the next set of functions. If it didn't, the results are investigated to find out what's wrong.

Such inspection should last a couple of hours at most. If at the end of this time, the programmer hasn't determined what's wrong, his time is better spent developing further tests to help isolate the difficulty than in continuing to stare at ambiguous test results.

8.2.2.1.1.4 Walkthroughs. Testing begins before the program is subjected to the computer. *Walkthroughs* of code detect bugs more efficiently than any other technique (Demarco, 1982, p. 222) and they also improve the quality of code.

8.2.2.1.1.5 Program Structure.   The best way to debug a program is to not introduce bugs in the first place. Structured programming contributes to this goal. It also makes the code easier to correct when bugs are detected. Finally, it results in quality code. The structure of a program is documented in a decision table or some type of flowchart before coding begins.

8.2.2.1.1.6 Forms and Terminal Dialogues.   But programs are only part of the constructed system. Also included are forms and/or terminal dialogues, and user and operations manuals.

Specimen forms should be tried out and approved by the user before the order for printed forms is made. Terminal dialogues should undergo this same type of testing before being accepted for incorporation into the system.

8.2.2.1.1.7 User Manuals.   User manuals should be reviewed and approved by the user before being printed. The review should include use of the manual in user training programs.

A user manual has five sections—input, output, processing, files, and *error handling.* The first four sections are adapted from the functional specifications as modified by the work done in these areas during design and construction. The section on error handling is compiled from the sections on the same subject in the program specifications of the modules making up the system. Thus, writing the user manual shouldn't be a big task.

8.2.2.1.1.8 Operations Manual.   The *operations manual* should be reviewed and approved by the computer center. As a final test, at the end of link testing, computer center personnel should use the operations manual to run the system in a simulation of production.

The operations manual is developed according to standards specified by the computer center. If they don't have standards, find out how they'd like to see the operations manual before developing it, so the resulting manual is as useful as possible to them.

8.2.2.1.2 Program Specifications.   A second construction control technique is program specifications. Let us explain what we mean.

Systems are divided into parts, which we call *modules.* A module is a program or subroutine. Associated with each module is a document that describes the module's functions and how it goes about performing its functions. This document goes by various titles such as program narrative and internal specifications. We call it the program specifications. A table of contents for program specifications is shown in Figure 8-4.

The ultimate justification for program specifications is that they're necessary

1. Input:
   a. Medium.
   b. Format.
   c. Organization and access method.
   d. Content.

2. Output:
   a. Medium.
   b. Format.
   c. Organization and access method.
   d. Content.

3. Tables:
   a. Format.
   b. Content.
   c. Use.

4. Processing:
   a. Tests on input fields.
   b. Output field source.

5. Error handling.

Figure 8-4. Program specifications contents.

to make the module maintainable. However, if program specifications are written as the first step in module development, they then act as a control on the programmer's performance. His job is to develop a module that conforms to program specifications. It's generally the case that, if the programmer knows what he's to do, he does it. If a programmer deliberately departs from program specifications in developing a module, his job should be explained to him. It should be necessary to make this explanation only once, in a performance review.

In some instances, program specifications are prepared in advance and given to a programmer when he's assigned to a module. As far as controlling the programmer's performance is concerned, the problem with this approach is whether the programmer understands the program specifications. The solution is to let the programmer absorb the program specifications and then discuss them with him to see if he understands them.

However, we prefer the opposite approach. First discuss the what and how of the module with the programmer; then let him write the program specifications for your review. This review may result in revisions that require reviews, and so on. But when the programmer has prepared program specifications of which you approve, you and the programmer then have a common understanding of the module he's to develop.

The objection is sometimes raised that asking the programmer to write program specifications is asking too much from him in terms of creativity. To determine the validity of this objection, let's take Figure 8-4 and review it section by section to see how much creativity is involved.

The first two sections of program specifications are descriptions of input and output. There's no creativity here. This information was developed during design. All that's required is to find the information in the design specifications.

The third section of program specifications is a description of the tables used. How much creativity is involved here is a matter of whether the tables are used exclusively by this module or are used in common by several modules. If a table is used in common, then its format, content, and use will have been specified during design. All that's required to incorporate the table's description in the program specifications is to find it in the design specifications.

If the table is unique to the module, the programmer has to determine its format, content, and use. But this isn't a special requirement. It's part of the programmer's job. All that's being asked is that he design the table at the time he writes the program specifications rather than wait until he writes the code.

The fourth section of program specifications is a description of the processing done. All processing is specified in the functional specifications. Writing the processing section of the program specifications is a matter of locating, in the functional specifications, the processing descriptions applicable to the module being specified.

The final section of program specifications is error handling. The programmer typically can't complete this section at the time program specifications are written. Generally, when developing program structure, unanticipated error situations are identified. Thus, this section is subject to update. However, the approach to error handling in the module should be thought out before further work on the module is done. Describing this approach in the program specifications causes this to happen.

Thus, writing program specifications isn't an exercise in creativity. It's a matter of collecting and organizing information plus thinking through error handling and table format, content, and use. If a person can't do this, his qualifications as a programmer are in doubt. Thus, there's no reason not to have programmers write program specifications. In fact, the opposite is the case—there's every reason why they should.

An approach to developing program specifications that reduces their size is as follows. Since much of the information in program specifications is material taken from design and functional specifications, instead of reproducing the information in the program specifications, the program specifications just refer to appropriate sections of the other documents. This approach has the added advantage of having each unit of information appear in one document only, which makes specifications change easier to document.

Some programmers object to writing program specifications because they maintain that they're programmers, not writers. This objection is invalid, also. We're not asking the programmer to write the great American novel. All we're asking is that he describe, in writing, what the program is to do and how it's to perform its functions. This task is an exercise in organizing information. If the programmer can't do this, once more his qualifications as a programmer are in question. If he needs help in the mechanics of writing, *Organizing And Documenting Data Processing Information,* by Thomas R. Gildersleeve (Hayden, 1977), provides guidance.

8.2.2.1.3 Conventions. A third construction control technique is *conventions.* For example, of the 11 programs in the payroll system described in Appendix 3, two are sorts, while eight of the remaining nine pass the master file. You can have a standard data description made for the master file, put it on the library, and require that every program passing the master file use the library description of the file. In so doing, you've *conventionalized* that part of the data division of the programs passing the master file; thus, for this part of the programs, your control is absolute. The data description can't be changed without your approval. If a programmer finds a bug in the description, you have the library version corrected. Once corrected, this latest version of the data description is automatically used by all programs passing the master file. Using precoded subroutines is another example of conventializing program development.

8.2.2.2 Design. Now, what control techniques should you use during design so team member performance produces the best design?

8.2.2.2.1. Design Review Committee. "Best" means the optimum compromise between the conflicting desires of the interested parties. Therefore, one control technique is to assure that all interested parties review the proposed design and discuss it with each other before collectively approving it. This is the concept of the *design review committee,* which is the essential design control technique and which we discussed in the chapter on project prerequisites.

8.2.2.2.2 Standards. Many of the viewpoints of the members of the design review committee can be anticipated to the extent that they can be documented and standardized. Thus, the computer center has *standards* as to what characteristics make a system acceptable from an operations point of view; the maintenance group has standards as to what characteristics make a system acceptable from a maintenance point of view; the internal auditors have standards as to what characteristics make a system acceptable from an auditing point of view; and the quality assurance group has standards as to what characteristics make a system acceptable from the point of view of both efficient facility utilization and system flexibility. System designers should either conform to these standards or justify and get clearance from interested parties for deviations. Thus, specification of standards is a second design control technique.

8.2.2.2.3 Alternatives. "Best" also means the best *alternatives* considered. Therefore, a third design control technique is to require system designers to develop alternative designs and have reasons why one is better than the others.

An approach for coming up with a comprehensive range of alternative designs is as follows:

1. Rough out the most brute force design.
2. Do the same for the most exotic.
3. Rough out designs that mark significant points in the continuum between the two extremes identified in steps (1) and (2).
4. Mix and match features from the designs identified until a candidate for best design emerges.

8.2.2.3 Functional Specification. Finally, what controls should you use during functional specification so the team members' performance results in agreement with the user as to what the system is to do?

8.2.2.3.1 Specifications Approval. User approval of the functional specifications is the final demonstration that such agreement has been reached and is the essential functional specification control technique. The need to get approval operates as a control on team members, encouraging them to adhere to good system analysis practice.

8.2.2.3.2 Involvement. For user approval to be meaningful, the user must participate actively at a high level during functional specification. Four ways to do this are

1. Have a company policy that spells out what the user's responsibilities in system development are.
2. Educate the user on his responsibilities and how to carry them out.
3. Make clear to the user the advantages to him of getting involved.
4. Make him feel at ease with you. For a description of how to do this, see the chapter on "Interpersonal Relations" in *Successful Data Processing System Analysis.*

8.2.2.4 General Control Techniques. There are two performance control techniques appropriate to functional specification, design, and construction:

1. *Intraproject communication.*
2. *Personnel selection.*

8.2.2.4.1 Intraproject Communication. When more than one person works on a job, the problem of whether the products of the individual efforts will fit together exists. If people talk to each other about their work, this problem is minimized.

One way to get team members to communicate is to hold *meetings*. Walk-throughs of programs, designs, and functional specifications are one type of meeting. In particular, if two team members aren't getting together to resolve an interface definition problem, a meeting between them (which you call and attend as an interested observer) may break the ice.

However, the best way to get people to talk to one another is to keep them physically close to one another. Analysts, designers and programmers shouldn't be encouraged to identify their work habitat in terms of a location. Instead, they should be encouraged to identify with their furniture. Then when a person is assigned to a team, he and his furniture are moved to where the other people working on the team are located.

Meetings and *seating plans* provide people with the opportunity to talk to one another. To maximize the probability that they talk constructively with one another on work issues, *orient* them to the job as a whole. Don't just pass out assignments. Show your team members what the project intends to accomplish and how their tasks fit into this project goal. And as developments occur that impact the project, keep them informed. All this has to do with team building, on which we say more in the chapter on motivation.

8.2.2.4.2 Personal Selection.   Your ability to select your project staff is limited; thus you must make do with the people provided.

However, difference in personnel performance are large—variations on the order of ten to one exist (Demarco, 1982, p. 207). Under such circumstances, there's the possibility that one of the people assigned to your project may detract more from project performance than he adds to it.

While you have little to say on who works on your project, you've complete say on who doesn't. If your plan calls for five people, and one of the people assigned you know to be a detractor, you can tell your manager that you'd rather run the project with four people than with five (including the detractor). If your manager refuses to take back the detractor, you can immunize your project from the detractor's influence by not assigning him work.

Similarly, if during the course of the project, it becomes apparent that one of the team members is a detractor, take him off the project. After this, you must repair the damage done. It's better to throw the detractor's work away and start over, rather than try to correct his work.

8.2.2.5 The Tickler File.   In the preceding sections, our procedure for determining the control techniques appropriate to a particular activity was to de-

termine the purpose of the activity, to determine what performance leads to achieving this purpose, and to then develop techniques that encourage the performance for which we're looking. Let's now apply this procedure to your job.

An aspect of your job is to be forward looking. You must anticipate the problems the project could run into, make plans to avoid these problems, communicate these plans to the people who are in a position to deliver the resources required to avoid the problems, and get commitments from these people on delivery of these resources. At the same time, you commit to deliveries that you and the project are to make.

Without some aid, you're not going to remember all these commitments. Yet it's crucial that you do so.

1. Your reputation depends on your ability to deliver on your commitments.
2. Your ability to avoid problems for your project depends on seeing that the commitments made to you are met.

The way to remember a commitment is to enter it in a file that reminds you of the commitment when the time comes for you to act. We call such a file a *tickler file*. It's also known as a follow-up file or suspense file.

A tickler file is organized by date. It may be a file of papers, a desk calendar, a month at a glance calendar, or a computer terminal. It's used as follows.

8.2.2.5.1 Commitments From You. Suppose you've agreed to make a presentation to a number of user personnel on Friday the 19th. You make a note of this fact and file it under Tuesday the 16th or Wednesday the 17th, so you get the reminder far enough in advance to give yourself time to prepare the presentation.

8.2.2.5.2 Commitments to You. Or suppose you've received a commitment from someone concerning delivery of information, equipment, personnel, supplies, what have you. Place an entry in your tickler file that reminds you to remind the person of his commitment far enough in advance so that he can deliver on schedule. Reminding people of their commitments is known as follow-up, and it's an essential part of getting delivery. Thus, getting delivery is a two step process:

1. Getting a commitment from a person to make delivery.
2. Following up with the person so he takes the steps necessary to make delivery.

Don't be obnoxious about following up. If Charlie made a commitment to deliver some information three weeks from next Friday and it will take him a week to prepare the information, talk to him a week and a half before his delivery date, preferably on another subject. Then casually mention that you're really looking forward to receiving the information a week from Friday. This reminds him that it's time to start working on putting the information together.

8.2.2.5.3 Making It Work.   A tickler file works if you do two things:

1. Make an entry in it each time you make a commitment or have a commitment made to you.
2. Look at it each day so it reminds you of the actions to be taken that day.

COMMUNICATION

Throughout this book we place ourselves in the project leader's position. In chapters four through eight, our perspective was to look into the project. Our concern was with planning, monitoring and controlling the project members' activities. These are the project leader's coordination responsibilities.

In this chapter we acknowledge that a project doesn't exist in a vacuum, but in a living, changing environment. Maintaining our position as project leader, we change our perspective and look out into the project's environment. Our concern is with the project leader's responsibilities regarding the relation between the project and its environment. We call these responsibilities the project leader's communication responsibilities.

Communication is a big word. In this book we restrict its use to the relation between a project and its environment. When we use the term communication in other ways in this book, we indicate the use by means of a modifier, such as intraproject communications.

Inhabitants of a project's environment are

1. Your manager.
2. Your user.
3. The computer center.
4. *Service organizations* (both in and out of the organization) supplying your project with support services.

To gain insight into your communication responsibilities, let's look at the relation between a group and its leader in general. The first question we might ask is why, when there's a group, is there always a leader? For a better understanding of this question, let's ask a more fundamental question, Why are there groups in the first place?

The answer is that people recognize that they can, as a group, attain goals beyond their reach as individuals. They collectively attain these goals by specializing their activities according to their skills and aptitudes. Thus, in the proverbial Indian tribe, the fat people do the fishing, the lean people do the hunting, and the wise people make the medicine.

If the specialized activities of the group members are to mesh in the drive toward their common goal, the activities must be coordinated. This coordination is done by the leader. Thus, the leader is the group member whose specialty is coordination.

At one time, coordination skills were the rarest of all skills. Then the leader was recognizable because he always had the most fur, the biggest cave, and the prettiest women. In today's technological world, coordination skills are no longer necessarily the rarest. Consequently, the leader is no longer necessarily the person with the largest salary and office.

Not only does the leader coordinate group activities; he's also the chief communicator between the group and its environment. Thus, the President of the United States coordinates domestic policy and is also the chief foreign officer. The pattern is ubiquitous. The question is, Why?

One factor is the "little green man syndrome." When the flying saucer settles to the ground and the little green man steps out, he says, "Take me to your leader." The outsider who wants to know something about a group's activities doesn't want to talk to just any group member. He wants to talk to the coordinator, since he assumes that the coordinator is the group member with the overall perspective of the group's activities. Thus, there are forces in a group's environment drawing the coordinator into communication.

But there are also forces within a group that push the coordinator into communication. Within a group, the members' specialized activities impinge on one another, and it's in these areas that the members look to their leader for coordination. From time to time, the specialized activities of a group member also impinge on the group's environment. Just as the group member looks to his leader to coordinate his activities with his fellow group members, he also looks to his leader for direction on his interface with the environment. The group members not only expect their leader to know what's going on in the group, but they also expect him to know what's going on in the environment.

A leader maintains his position through the consent of the governed. If the group members don't feel their leader is in adequate communication with the environment—so his knowledge of circumstances is limited—a credibility gap arises, and the group may reject the leader's coordination. President Johnson's decision to not seek a second term is an example of how a group can turn its leader out.

If you want to do an effective job of coordinating, you must pay attention to your communication responsibilities—for the two are mutually dependent, and you can't neglect one without degrading the other.

As a project leader, you must maintain a balance between communication and coordination. If you concentrate on coordination to the exclusion of communication, you become progressively out of touch with what's going on in the environment, and ultimately, your coordination becomes unreal and ineffective. On the other hand, if you concentrate on communication to the exclusion of coordination, you become progressively out of touch with what's going on in your project, and ultimately, you cease to have anything about which to communicate.

Most of us with a programming and design background appreciate the importance of coordination, but the initial reaction of many of us to communication is that it's an interruption, a distraction, and a waste of time. Given our background, this attitude is understandable. When we were programmers, we were given well-bounded problems requiring long periods of concentration to solve. When we became designers, the size of the problems with which we wrestled became larger, but the work didn't change—it was still a matter of solving the problem within set boundaries, and it still required long periods of concentration. Now, when we become project leaders and are given a project goal to achieve, our reaction is frequently, "OK, you've given me a job to do. Now leave me alone so I can do it."

Unfortunately, the attitude that served well for programming and design isn't functional for project management. When we receive an invitation to communicate, we must stifle our negative reaction and, instead, consider the invitation an opportunity to deepen our understanding of the context in which our project operates.

This doesn't mean you accept every invitation to communicate that is offered. You must maintain a balance between communication and coordination; you've plenty of coordination responsibilities, and therefore, the amount of time you can devote to communication is limited. What you want is to participate in those communications that are productive, both for you and the people with whom you are communicating, and turn down the invitations to communication which is going to be unproductive, particularly for you. (Communication is *productive* for you if it furthers your understanding of the environment in which your project operates and that, consequently, increases your coordination effectiveness.)

You don't have to worry about getting invitations to communicate. If you dispense meaningful information in an understandable way, the "little green man syndrome" guarantees that you'll get invitations to communicate. The problem is: How do you tell which invitations to accept and which to decline at the time the invitations are offered?

9.1 AVOIDING UNPRODUCTIVE MEETINGS

One type of communication is meetings. If you could tell beforehand which meetings to attend and which to avoid, you'd save time. Fortunately, there are tests to help you distinguish the gold from the dross.

There's only one legitimate reason for calling a meeting—to get the attendees to agree on the next step to take toward the solution of a common problem. This is called the *purpose* of the meeting.

Not every meeting has a purpose. For example, sometimes a meeting is called just because "we haven't had a meeting for a while."

The invitation to a meeting should state the meeting's purpose, so the attendees can prepare themselves to participate. If an invitation doesn't state the meeting's purpose, you can't be faulted for getting in touch with the person who has called the meeting and saying, "Charlie, I got your invitation to the meeting next Tuesday. Thank you very much. I'd like to contribute to your meeting as much as possible, and I'm wondering if you can tell me the meeting's purpose, so I can prepare myself." If the person calling the meeting doesn't know its purpose, you can always say that you've a previous commitment next Tuesday.

Once you've ascertained the meeting's purpose, decide if you can contribute. If you can, you should attend the meeting. It's an opportunity for you to help the other attendees, and such meetings are the ones most likely to produce information you can use in doing your job.

People are sometimes invited to meetings that have a purpose, but to which they can't contribute. For example, technical people are sometimes invited to meetings on the off chance that some technical question may arise. This isn't sufficient justification for tying down such people for the length of the meeting.

If after you've determined the purpose of the meeting, you can't see how you can contribute, you can hardly be condemned for saying, "OK, Charlie, that certainly is a good reason for having a meeting. But frankly, I don't quite see how I fit in. In what way can I contribute?" If Charlie's reason for your attendance isn't attractive, you can once more consider begging off on the basis of a previous commitment. For example, if the only reason you're invited is because Charlie feels there's some remote chance that, sometime during the meeting, someone might raise a question only you can answer, then you can reply, "Charlie, I can see how I might be of help to you in that regard. Unfortunately, I'm all tied up next Tuesday. But I'll be here in the office, and if a question does come up, please call me. I'd be glad to take time out to give you the answer."

Don't hesitate to plead a previous commitment if you don't want to attend a meeting you feel will be unproductive. You're not lying. As project leader, you've plenty of commitments, and while the meeting is being held, you'll be tied up with one of them. Of course, when you tell someone that you've a previous commitment, he'll think you have a prior appointment, although you may not. But you never said that you had a prior appointment, only a prior commitment.

Since meetings chew up time, avoiding unproductive meetings when your co-ordination responsibilities demand can be justified. But again, what we're describing here is a tool, in this case a tool to use your time effectively. Use the tool with judgment. If your manager calls a meeting without a stated purpose, it's appropriate to inquire after the purpose, so you can prepare. But go, even if you don't think you can contribute. And if other pressures aren't overwhelming, go to the meetings to which you're invited even if you don't think that they'll be productive. You don't want to create the impression that you're uncooperative. And you may be able to build up your political capital.

If on a given day, there's something you have to do and can't afford interruptions, hide. If you've an office with a door and a secretary, close the door and tell your secretary that you don't want to be disturbed. Of course, have her screen your messages so your manager can get through.

However, if you don't have these facilities, take a more extreme approach. Gather up what you need to get your work done and move to an unoccupied office, an unused meeting room, or the library.

9.2 HANDLING POTENTIALLY DISRUPTIVE COMMUNICATIONS

A type of communication between you and your user that we've already discussed is requests for change. Requests for change are an example of a *potentially disruptive* form of *communication*. By *disruptive*, we mean disruptive to your ability to carry out your coordination responsibilities. A request for change is disruptive when it's communicated to a project member and he agrees to make the change. As a consequence, the specifications as this project member sees them and the specifications as they appear to you and the other project members now differ, and this difference creates a coordination problem for you.

One way to control the disruptive effects of requests for change is to *channel* them. That is, you tell the user all requests for change are to be submitted to you. And you tell the project members that, if any member of the user organization makes a request for change to any one of them, he's to

1. Listen politely.
2. Make no commitments.
3. After the member of the user organization has left, come to you and describe what has happened.

You take it from there.

Another way to control the disruptive effects of requests for change is to *formalize* them. Design a form on which they're to be submitted, and establish a procedure for processing the form.

As we've already pointed out, you don't use either of these approaches unless called for. If the user is channeling his requests for change to you, setting up procedures to see that he continues to do so is insulting and counterproductive. But if the user is going around you to the project members, setting up a channel for requests for change is appropriate. And if the frequency of requests for change is getting out of hand, then formalize the request procedure.

In general, if you find a type of communication that's disrupting your coordination responsibilities, two ways to control it are to channel it and formalize it. In giving this advice, we're encouraging you to establish a bureaucracy. As long as this bureaucracy performs a positive function, fine. The trouble with bureaucracies is that they hang on after the need for them disappears. So when you establish a bureaucracy, do a favor for those who come after—make clear why you established the bureaucracy. And if the need for it goes away, do away with it.

9.3 STATUS REPORTS

You may be requested to submit status reports to your manager and/or your user. A status report is a periodic written report on the status of your project.

9.3.1 The Function Of Status Reports

The purpose of a status report is to provide the recipient with the information he needs to control your performance—that is, to know where interventions are necessary and where operations are proceeding well enough so managerial time and energy can be devoted elsewhere. To the extent possible, you should try to satisfy this purpose when preparing status reports. However, there are two qualifications.

The first qualification is that your status reports contain no surprises. That is, if a development occurs on your project which either your manager or user would consider significant, don't wait until status report time to communicate with respect to the development. Tell the interested parties right away.

You should recognize most project developments about which your manager or user wants to know, and if you keep them informed as you should, submitting status reports is largely redundant. However, the second qualification now comes into play.

The second qualification is that status reports perform a more important function for you than they do for the recipient. Preparing status reports forces you to review the progress of your project to date, assess this progress in terms of your project goal and plan, and adjust your plan appropriately to maintain your best posture toward your project goal. This function is important, because as the saying goes, when you're up to your ass in alligators, it's hard to remember that your purpose is to drain the swamp.

The nature of project management is that there's always a crisis de jour demanding your attention. Without some constraint to cause you to do otherwise, it's easy to slip into a continuous mode of killing alligators. The periodic need to prepare a status report provides this constraint. Let's look at status reports from this point of view and see if we can determine what a status report should cover.

9.3.2 The Plan Review

In preparing a status report, the first thing you do is develop a list of accomplishments that have occurred since submission of your last report. This list consists of all checkpoints and deadlines met during the last report period and represents your progress during this period.

Next, you evaluate your progress during the last report period against the goals set for the period, which in turn, gives you a picture of where you now stand in terms of your project goal and plan.

In making this evaluation, you'll pinpoint *problems* (contingencies) of various types:

1. Problems that have occurred and which have set you back, but which have subsequently been solved.
2. Problems that have occurred and which are setting you back, but for which you have solutions, which are being implemented.
3. Problems that have occurred, which are setting you back, which are beyond your control, and for which you've suggested solutions which have not yet been implemented.

Once you've enumerated your accomplishments, evaluated your progress toward your project goal, and identified your problems, you're ready to develop your short-term plans for maintaining your best posture toward your project goal. These plans take the form of *short-term goals* to be reached during the next report period or shortly thereafter.

While you're formulating these short-term goals, you'll anticipate problems that may arise in attaining these goals. These will be problems that are beyond your control and will be some form of delivery failure.

Once you've taken the steps described above, you'll have thoroughly reviewed your project; that is, you'll have acknowledged things that you were previously either unaware of or unwilling to admit; and you'll have collected a comprehensive set of status information in the following categories:

1. Accomplishments in the last report period.
2. Progress toward the project goal.
3. Short-term goals.
4. Problems
   a. Now solved but which have set you back, with a note of the delay introduced.
   b. Being solved, with a note of the delay experienced so far.
   c. Beyond your control and for which you've suggested a solution, with a note of the delay experienced so far.
   d. Anticipated as potentially setting back short-term goals.

Once you've completed this review, you've completed your ongoing job of planning. You can now go back to the day to day concerns of project management with a finer understanding, of where you are and where you want to go, to guide you.

9.3.3 The Project History

Even if no one wants a status report, document the information collected in your *periodic plan review*. Organize this document under the topics of accomplishments, overall progress, immediate future goals, and problems, and organize the sections on problems under the subtopics of solved, being solved, beyond your control, and anticipated.

A collection of these periodic plan review documents constitutes your *project history*. No other record keeping for historical purposes is necessary.

This raises the question: Is there any reason why a project history should be kept? In the course of your work as project leader, you'll find that, on occasion, you'll want to reconstruct what happened at some prior point in the life of your project. Without a project history, your reconstruction is going to be partial. This need alone is sufficient justification for a project history. Later in this chapter, we discuss a second use for a project history.

Finally, your manager may require you to keep a project history. If he does, try to convince him that it should be kept in the format described above. If he insists on a different format, comply, but try to make the contents of the history delineate accomplishments, overall progress, immediate future plans, and problems in all their detail on a periodic basis.

9.3.4 Writing The Report

If your manager or user wants status reports, then you want him to read them, for three reasons:

1. If your status reports keep the recipient informed, this can only increase his desire to aid you when you need help (which is constantly).

2. Status reports are an opportunity to remind the recipient of problems, whose solutions lie in his hands. He won't be reminded if he doesn't read your reports.
3. Status reports are a vehicle for documenting decisions made with respect to your project.

Your periodic plan review document provides the basis for a status report. However, it contains too much information, and your user will find the bulk of this information irrelevant. Even your manager will be interested in selected portions only. Since people aren't interested in reading reports containing irrelevant information, customize your reports to the recipients.

This is a special case of the general problem of report writing. Writing reports is a two step procedure:

1. Collect the information.
2. Organize the information so the recipient will read the report.

So how should a status report be organized? Your periodic-plan-review document should appear as a set of appendices on accomplishments, overall progress, immediate future plans, and problems in all their variety. The report should be a page, or two at the most, that highlights the information in the appendices. As we've already said, one thing you want to highlight is problems, the solutions to which lie in the recipient's hands. But you don't want the recipient to view the report as bad news only, since this won't encourage him to read it. Highlight the good news also, specifically, the accomplishments representing progress toward his goals. And be sure decisions made are included.

The best format for your status report is tabloid. Cover each subject in one or, at most, two sentences, and surround each subject with lots of space. Use of bullets effects this kind of report organization.

Your user's report should be different than your manager's, since they have different concerns. The report by itself is sufficient for your user. The appendices should be attached to your manager's report, for even though he'll never look at them all, after reading your report, he may want to selectively review them.

Writing a status report to your user may create a political problem in that there may be things your manager doesn't want your user to know. If this is the case, draft your user's status report and have your manager approve it before issuing it. If you write a status report that your user looks forward to, you won't have a problem getting a timely review by your manager. Your manager doesn't want the user making noises about where his status report is.

Some project leaders take the following approach to status report preparation. They ask each project member to prepare a status report to the project leader. They then combine these reports to make up a status report for the user or manager. This approach is wrong on two counts:

1. If you need status reports from project members to find out what's going on, you're too far away from your project to manage it effectively.
2. The approach avoids the need for a periodic plan review, which is the prime reason for status reporting.

9.3.5 Report Frequency

The next question is: How frequently should a status report be prepared? If you're leading a project such as the payroll project we've been using as a case study, and if you do everything we've described above to conduct a periodic plan review, it will take a day or two to do the review. You can't do this review too frequently, or you won't have enough time for your other responsibilities.

Therefore, conduct a plan review once a month. If company procedures require you to submit a status report more frequently, submit interim, exception reports as updates to a comprehensive monthly report.

If you conduct a plan review once a month, take notes during the month, because at the end of the month you aren't going to remember everything significant that has happened during the month. We aren't suggesting anything fancy. A manila folder in which you drop notes when significant things happen is sufficient. Many significant events come accompanied by documents, and in this case, you don't have to make notes. Just drop a copy of the document in your folder. If it's necessary to write a note, the note doesn't have to be comprehensive—just a few words to remind you of the event is sufficient. The object isn't to develop a well-organized, easily readable historical document, but simply to assemble a collection of notes which assures that you consider all pertinent information in your next plan review.

9.4 AVOIDING UNNECESSARY REPORT WRITING

Now and then, project leaders are asked to prepare special reports. For example, the data processing director may give a member of his staff the assignment to investigate the extent to which the system development department meets its deadlines. Consequently, as part of his information collecting effort, the staff person asks you to prepare a report on the deadlines set up on your project; the extent to which they're met; and where deadlines have been missed, by how much they have been missed and why. The data processing director is within his rights to initiate this investigation, and his staff person is justified in asking for this information.

Once more, use judgment. If you can prepare the report, do so. Your project history makes this an easy job.

But if you're in a crack and can't spare the time, you can give a copy of your project history to the staff person and tell him that

1. You'd like to prepare the report but don't have the time
2. The information for which he's looking can be extracted from the project history
3. If he needs help in extracting this information, you'd be happy to answer questions.

Without a project history, you're in a bind. You can't palm off the staff person with a copy of your project history, so you must prepare the report. And this won't be easy, because you don't have a project history as a source for your report data.

9.5 SERVICE ORGANIZATIONS

The term, *service organization*, covers a spectrum of organizations including consultants, hardware manufacturers, proprietary software houses, and publishers. One thing these organizations have in common is that they're in the same position with respect to you as you are with respect to your user. Therefore, if you run into a problem dealing with one of these organizations and don't know how to handle it, a general approach is to think of the most similar situation your user could be in relation to you and ask yourself how your user would attack the problem. Thus, you contract for the services of a service organization; you define your needs; if necessary, you enter a phased development procedure with the service organization; you request a status report, so the service organization has to make a periodic plan review; you require that you be kept abreast of developments; you set deadlines; you keep the service organization notified of your changes in plans and requirements; and so on. And in dealing with service organizations, always remember the major complaint you have of users— they don't get involved at a high level. Don't be a poor user.

9.6 THE COMPUTER CENTER

Communicating with the computer center occurs in two contexts:

1. With respect to testing, the computer center is a service organization. Communicate with it accordingly.
2. The computer center will run the system you're developing. How well the system runs in production is one measure of your performance; so do what it takes to see that the system runs smoothly. Design the system so it fits into the computer center's schedule. Develop a useful operations manual, and deliver it early enough for the computer center to become familiar with

the system. See that computer center personnel get the training they need to run the system. See that the center is informed of the supplies and facilities it will need to support your system, and see that they're informed early enough so orders can be placed in time for delivery before the dry run of the system (so the dry run can be as realistic as possible). And do these things by coordinating with the computer center manager or the organization he's put in place to accept new systems. Don't alienate the computer center by walking past its management and procedures to tell computer center personnel what they should do.

MOTIVATION

A major resource used in all phases of system development is personnel. As a project leader, you attain your goal by getting your project members to complete their tasks successfully—that is, on time and with quality. People perform differently depending on the environment in which they work. Creating and maintaining an environment that encourages people to complete their tasks successfully is the goal of motivation, and consequently, you can't divorce yourself from the need to motivate.

We've dealt with people all our lives and we know that they react better in some situations than in others. We also have some idea how to bring about these situations. The purpose of this chapter is to clarify these concepts and encourage you to use them.

It takes a lot of enjoyable and successful cooperative activity to build a good relationship with a person, but it takes only one harsh word or thoughtless act to establish a bad relationship. No one expects you to be perfect, and if you've demonstrated a consistently sincere attempt to get along with people, your gaffs will tend to be forgiven and forgotten. Nevertheless, in every human relations situation, there's something that can be done to improve the relationship and something that can be done to harm it. These can be referred to as the right and wrong things to do. Although it's often easier to do the wrong thing, you must exercise the self-control to do the right thing.

10.1 DEFINITION

We now define motivation. You may not be happy with our definition, since it's a definition by exclusion. However, we adopt it because it's the most realistic definition we've found. The definition is as follows:

> Performance is influenced by individual differences in personality and intelligence. Improvement in performance comes with training and experience. However, when all differences in personality, intelligence, training and experience have been taken into account, there is left a residue of unexplained performance. This residue is called "motivation."

One claim the data processing community has to this definition is that it was formulated by one of its members, Gerry Weinberg, in his book, The Psychology Of Computer Programming (pp. 180, 181, Van Nostrand Reinhold, 1971).

10.2 EXPECTANCY THEORY

An appealing motivational theory is *expectancy theory*. Its tenets are as follows:

1. The best performers see their jobs in terms of *clear performance goals*. They believe they can perform well with respect to these goals, and they see a strong relationship between performing well and getting the *rewards* they value. These rewards are of two types:
   a. *Extrinsic* rewards—Rewards given to the person by his environment.
   b. *Intrinsic* rewards—Rewards the person gives himself.
2. *Job satisfaction* has to do with the *congruence* between the rewards a person sees himself receiving and the rewards he thinks he should receive.
   a. The rewards a person thinks he should receive are a direct function of
      i) What he thinks the job requires in the way of skills, abilities, and training.
      ii) How he perceives the demands of the job—its difficulty and the responsibilities for which it calls.
   b. The rewards a person sees himself receiving are
      i) A direct function of the rewards he receives.
      ii) An inverse function of the rewards he sees his *comparative others* (people with whom he compares himself) receiving.
3. There's no relation between *performance* and job satisfaction. That is, a person can be dissatisfied with his job and still perform well, or satisfied with his job and perform poorly. But job satisfaction is inversely related to voluntary absenteeism and turnover.

10.3 INTRINSIC REWARDS

One of the things expectancy theory emphasizes is that part of the rewards a person gets from his job are *intrinsic*, that is, rewards he gives himself. The concept of intrinsic rewards ties in with the idea that, if you give people the opportunity, they provide their own motivation for doing their tasks.

10.3.1 Satisfying Interests

Different people bring different *interests* to their jobs—some look for responsibility, some for the opportunity to learn new skills, some for the challenge of a previously unsolved problem, some for security, and so on. If you allow the person to shape his tasks to his interests, one aspect of your motivation problem is solved. Part of this shaping involves assigning tasks that fit a person's interests. But tasks can be approached in a variety of ways. If task assignments are not overspecified, the person assigned the task can see it from his point of view.

For example, given the chance, a person may interpret a maintenance task as an opportunity to learn how a particular data processing problem is solved. However, if you convey the impression that maintenance is scut work, a large part of the person's opportunity to motivate himself is destroyed. Or when assigned a task similar to one just completed, if not given the impression that such an assignment is dullsville, a person may consider it an opportunity to refine skills learned on the previous task. A striking illustration of this type of motivation is as follows.

An installation was converting from one computer to another. It had 200 Fortran programs that were instrumental to installation operation. The Fortran language specifications for the new computer varied from those for the computer being replaced. Consequently, each Fortran program had to be inspected and modified to run on the replacement computer. One person was assigned this job.

Here was a prime example of an apparently boring job. Having modified one program, the programmer had only 199 more programs for which to make similar modifications. But this programmer had systems programming interests. Consequently, his approach to the job was to study the two sets of language specifications and build a translator that would automatically modify the 200 programs. By not having his job assignment overspecified, the programmer was able to cast it into a frame that interested him. A potentially deadening assignment was transformed into a stimulating and educational experience.

Don't let this example give you the impression that shaping a task to one's interests is always biased toward creativity. For example, if you felt that the way to convert the 200 Fortran programs was to build a translator and you gave the job of building the translator to a person who preferred to work through the programs and correct them one by one, you'd be guilty of overspecifying the job assignment.

10.3.2 Sense Of Accomplishment

Another reason for not overspecifying task assignments is that people want to work on assignments they consider their own. They want a *sense of accomplishment*. As a project leader, you must retain control over what's done. But if you not only tell people what to do, but also how to do it, they can't think of themselves as individuals using their skills to carry out assignments—they can only consider themselves tools that you're using to reach your goal.

Most of us have little difficulty passing out responsibility at the time task assignments are made, since we recognize that delegation of these responsibilities is the only way to achieve our goal. But as work progresses and we discover that project members are carrying out their assignments in ways different from the way we'd have approached them, it's difficult to refrain from suggesting our approach. Yet we must. For any suggestion on our part assumes some aspect of an order. And making such suggestions demonstrates that we didn't give the project members responsibility for their assignments after all—we're really retaining it ourselves.

A paradigm for making suggestions is as follows:

1. A project member is carrying out an assignment differently than you would, but it looks like his approach will work. Under these circumstances you should keep your peace, and let the project member pursue his approach.
2. The project member is making mistakes, but they're of such a nature that he'll recognize them and recover from them. Once more you should keep your peace. The project member will learn more and get a greater sense of accomplishment if he finds and corrects his errors himself. Remember: The right to make decisions is the right to make mistakes.
3. The project member is making mistakes that will mire him in difficulties if he's allowed to go on. Your approach should be as follows:
   a. By means of a discussion, get the project member to recognize the problem. Your part in the discussion is to ask questions such as "What happens if . . .?" By answering these questions, the project member is allowed to discover the problem.
   b. Once the project member recognizes the problem, be quiet. The object is to get the project member to suggest a solution to the problem. If you've been successful in convincing the project member that the task is his responsibility, he won't hestitate to do so.
   c. Proposed solutions that don't solve the problem are handled the same way as the original problem. That is, if the proposed solution involves

difficulties, ask the project member questions which cause him to find the difficulties.

d. Eventually, the project member will suggest a solution that's at least as good as any you could have proposed. But the real benefit of this approach is that, throughout the discussion, the project member makes the decisions (all you've done is ask questions), and he has every right to continue to consider his assignment his responsibility.

The technique described in item (3) above is called *participative decision making*, and it can be used in all situations where a person isn't prepared to be given full responsibility for a task.

However, running a participative decision making session isn't easy. You must be knowledgeable in the area in which the decision is to be made; otherwise, you won't be able to guide the discussion. Ideally, you should have a solution in mind when the discussion begins. But you must be flexible enough to adjust if the project member takes an approach different from yours.

You probably recognize that the procedure we recommended for working with a project member who proposes what you consider to be unrealistic checkpoints is an example of the use of participative decision making.

Participative decision making also gives you insight into a project member's capabilities.

The concept of having the project member consider his assignment his responsibility isn't a game you play only until the project member completes his assignment. The delegation is forever. Thus, any credit for a task well done must always go to the project member. If not, he'll feel duped, and your credibility will suffer.

10.4 CLEAR PERFORMANCE GOALS

A second thing emphasized by expectancy theory is that, to get good performance from a person, he must have clear performance goals. Up to now in this chapter we've concentrated on task assignments, which are an aspect of performance goals. But a job involves more than just completing tasks. People want to feel that they've performed on the job in general. To do this, they must know what good performance is. Consequently, make your performance *expectations* clear. Task assignments and checkpoints are two aspects of performance that we've already discussed. Other aspects are

1. When the working day starts.
2. How time cards are filled in and when they're turned in.
3. What procedures are followed. Examples of procedures are
   a. When and how interviews are documented.
   b. What constitutes program structure and how it's documented.
   c. What a unit test plan consists of and when it's prepared.

Of help in this area are installation standards. However, the lack of such standards doesn't relieve you of the responsibility to make your expectations clear to your project members.

It would be nice if your position on all issues could be demonstrated to be correct, but such isn't the case. Some issues have partisans, pro and con. Whether people get to work on time is such an issue. Some project leaders are indifferent to tardiness, while some aren't. Who's correct isn't a question we want to get into here. If you feel that project members should get to work on time and you use their punctuality as one basis for judging performance, you can probably maintain this position. But make your project members aware of your attitude, so they can adjust their performance accordingly.

10.4.1 Personal Adherence

One aspect of making your expectations clear is to adhere to them. Project members won't consider a procedure important if you don't follow it. Moreover, if you don't adhere to a procedure but mark down your project members for not following it, they'll feel cheated. Once more, your credibility suffers.

10.4.2 Giving Credit

A second aspect of making expectations clear is to *give credit* when your expectations are met. Some of us are too sparing with credit, reserving it for outstanding achievement only. If people just do their jobs, we ask, "Why is this deserving of credit? They only did what they were supposed to." But isn't this what we want? And therefore, isn't credit due? Be sure your allocation of credit encourages performance you want. Reserving credit for outstanding performance gives the impression that acceptable performance isn't worthy and leads to an attitude of, "Who cares, anyhow?"

The classic example of credit misallocation is as follows. On the day the payroll is to be run, a bug is discovered in the calculation program. Charlie, who wrote the program, dives in to find the bug and fix it. He works all day, eats supper at his desk, and labors far into the night. Finally, at 2 A.M., Charlie finds the bug, the program is fixed, the system is run, and the paychecks are printed just in time for payday. Obviously, Charlie deserves credit. But how about the five other programmers who also worked on the payroll system and used testing techniques that precluded a production breakdown? Did they receive credit? Or were they just doing their job? And which kind of performance is more desirable, anyway?

10.4.3 Performance Review

A third aspect of making expectations clear is to help people improve their performance when it fails to meet expectations. This brings up the subject of performance review. Performance review isn't a periodic responsibility of yours; it's continuous. The time to talk to a project member about his performance failure is when it becomes habitual. An occasional failure isn't grounds for reviewing a project members performance. The project member frequently recognizes his failure, and his efforts to improve has better results than anything you can do. However, repeated failure indicates that the project member doesn't recognize his performance as substandard. Then a performance review is appropriate.

Rules for conducting performance reviews are as follows:

1. Hold the review in private. The project member may not be aware that his performance isn't satisfactory. Point out his shortcomings in private so he can improve without being publicly embarrassed.
2. Schedule the review so there's plenty of time to hold it. The review shouldn't be rushed.
3. Make arrangements so nothing interrupts the review. The project member's performance is of prime importance to him, and you should demonstrate that it's of prime importance to you, too.
4. Use the "sandwich" technique—that is, sandwich unfavorable remarks between favorable ones. Compliment the project member at the beginning and end of the review.
5. Be objective. Cite instances of performance failure.
6. Allow the project member to express his reaction to your evaluation. Give him the opportunity to state what obstacles stand in the way of his doing a good job. Here you may find the underlying cause of unsatisfactory performance. If you're asked for advice, don't be quick to give your opinion. Let the project member talk. Ask him questions. Sometimes the first problem he mentions isn't the basic problem.
7. Don't show anger or hostility, regardless of what the project member says. Nobody says you can't lose your temper now and then, but do it some time other than when you're conducting a review.
8. Don't be determined to prove the project member wrong. Help him save face, and leave his self-respect intact. Confidence in you is increased if the project member realizes that you aren't arbitrary and that incorrect evaluations can be changed.
9. Take your time. It may be a while before the project member admits his errors, and it's unlikely that he'll agree with your criticisms during the review. When criticized, most people rise to their defense. Don't let this bother you. Make your points and listen to what the project member has to say. Then conclude the review and see if his performance improves. A person will sometimes take your advice even though he denied everything you said in the review. This change in performance is what you're interested in. Whether he agrees with you verbally is immaterial.

10. If the project member wants to talk, let him go. Don't interrupt.
11. If you feel it's necessary to bring up a personality shortcoming, be specific. If you can't pinpoint how an alleged personality fault causes a performance failure, it's better not to venture into this area.

A performance review has several possible outcomes:

1. Performance improves.
2. Performance doesn't improve. Under such circumstances, another performance review is held.
   a. If the project member is interested in improving his performance, a series of performance reviews may succeed where one has failed.
   b. If the project member isn't interested in improving his performance, a series of performance reviews generally convinces him that he isn't going to get ahead on your project. Usually, such people eventually quit to look for greener pastures. Departure of such a person may cause a temporary inconvenience, but in the long run, both your project and your organization are better off. Here we see the seamless connection between motivation and *discipline*.
   c. If after a series of reviews, a person's performance doesn't improve and he doesn't voluntarily move on, you must try to convince him of the impossibility of the situation. If he's willing to agree with you, help him find another position in which he'll feel more at home. If he doesn't agree, however, you must take him off the project. Any other action demonstrates to the other project members that performance doesn't count. Once more, we see the inseparability of motivation and discipline.

10.5 REWARD CONGRUENCE

In every organization, there's a system of rewards involving raises, promotions, and opportunities. Not only do people want the self-satisfaction of accomplishment, they also want to see their performance recognized. Expectancy theory points out this fact by observing that people experience job satisfaction only when they see a congruence between rewards deserved and rewards received.

Such congruence is the case only if the reward system passes out raises, promotions, and opportunities in proportion to level of performance. As a project leader, it isn't your prerogative to distribute these rewards; this is done by your manager. However, you're the person who's most knowledgeable about your project members' performance, and your manager makes his reward decisions on the basis of the appraisals you make of this performance. These appraisals must be written, and if the reward system is to reflect performance, your appraisals must be honest. They must describe both the project members' achievements and failings.

For the project members to have confidence in the reward system, each project member must be privy to his *performance appraisal*. This is the reason the appraisal must be written. Then the project member sees the same appraisal as does your manager.

Another reason for letting the project member read the written performance appraisal is that, under such circumstances, you are going to exercise care when you choose the words which will go into the project member's personnel record.

Nothing in a project member's performance appraisal should come as a surprise to him. If there's anything negative in the appraisal, he should have heard about it several times in the performance reviews you've previously held with him.

10.6 BUILDING A TEAM

Not overspecifying task assignments; a clear broadcast of your performance expectations; the giving of credit; the conduct of timely, constructive performance reviews; and the submission of honest performance appraisals represent an area of motivation having to do with creating a work environment in which each project member's self-motivation has an opportunity to experience maximum sway. Another major area of motivation has to do with developing a *team*. A team accomplishes more than the same individuals working on separate tasks.

A member of a group recognizes himself as such because he has more in common with the other group members than he has with people who aren't members—his attitudes are more like his fellow group members, he knows more about them, he talks with them more, he does more things with them, and he's physically nearer to them. All these commonalities are ways you can engender a team feeling.

1. Use the project goal to generate among the project members the attitude of a team working toward a common goal. One way of generating this attitude is to keep everyone informed as to what's going on.
   a. Each project member's orientation includes, not only what he's going to do, but also what the project goal is and what each project member's role is in attaining this goal.
   b. It's not necessary for each project member to have a copy of all project documentation, but a set of this documentation should be available if a project member wants to refer to it.
   c. Circulate a copy of each status report you prepare among the project members so they can keep abreast of project progress.
   d. Although a specifications change may affect the work of only some project members, make all members aware of the change so no one feels left out.

e. Every question a project member asks about the project deserves a thorough answer, even if the answer has no bearing on the work of the project member asking the question. That he asked the question indicates that he's identifying with the project rather than with his assignment. Encourage such identification.

2. One way to disseminate information is through meetings. Also, meetings bring project members close physically. Walkthroughs are an example of this team building technique.

3. An even better way to establish physical proximity is to seat project members next to each other.

4. Such a seating arrangement also encourages project members to talk with one another.

10.7 WORKING CONDITIONS

A third area of motivation is concerned with *working conditions*. Any part of the project members' work environment that helps them do their work is motivating; any part that introduces interruption and delay is demotivating. Thus, you should see that office facilities are adequate—that there are enough desks, chairs, terminals, wastepaper baskets, filing cabinets, bookcases, phones, and calendars; that there are adequate stationery supplies such as tablets of lined paper, coding paper, pencils, pens, and templates; that there's sufficient clerical support; that adequate computer time is available; that training is provided; that distractions are minimized; etc. Once more, what we're talking about is your responsibility to keep down contingencies. A person who's expected to meet a deadline under a continuous barrage of interruptions and delays will struggle for just so long. After that, his attitude degenerates into one of, "Oh, well, What's the use of trying?"—the antithesis of being motivated. Expectancy theory emphasises this motivational responsibility by pointing out that, to perform well, a person must feel he's capable of meeting the performance goals making up his job.

10.8 GIVING DIRECTION

The final area of motivation with which we deal is your role as leader. Every project member is a specialist in some aspect of the project. The project members leave it to you to coordinate their specialized activities to arrive at the project goal. As a consequence, whenever a project member confronts a problem that extends beyond his specialization, he'll come to you for guidance. If *direction* isn't forthcoming, the project member is left in an ambiguous situation, in which motivation tends to wane. Expectancy theory emphasizes the importance of such direction. It's a part of giving your project members clear performance goals.

These facts have several implications for the way you carry out your role:

1. You must be available, both physically and in terms of attitude, so project members can bring their problems to you.
2. You must be sure the requests for direction which project members bring to you lie outside their responsibilities. Some people may bring you problems that are within the bounds of their assignments and which they should resolve themselves. Rather than give direction in these areas, you must return such problems to your people unsolved and with the understanding that they have the right, privilege, and responsibility to resolve these problems.
3. However, when a problem is beyond a project member's task assignment, you must render a decision promptly. This doesn't mean you must make snap decisions—it does mean that, after a reasonable time for reflection (a day or two, at most), direction must be forthcoming.

The need for direction often arises at conflict points in system development— what a project member wants conflicts with the desires of the user, the computer center, or some other outside group. Or it conflicts with what some other project member is doing. The need to give direction at these conflict points presents you with both a benefit and a danger. The benefit is that, by becoming involved in the resolution of these conflicts, you remain abreast of the most important aspects of the system development going on in your project.

The danger is that, because the conflict is between the needs and desires of two or more parties, resolution of the conflict may result in personal disappointment. The way to minimize this danger is to get the conflicting parties to participate with you in resolving the problem. Your role in the discussion is to keep everyone's attention focused on the project goal. If you've been successful in generating a team approach to system development, you should be able to get the conflicting parties to resolve their difficulties within the context of the project goal and, thus, minimize disappointment.

The most important thing to do when a project member comes to you with a problem is listen. Sometimes the only thing he needs is a sounding board. As a consequence, with a few questions on your part, or sometimes nothing more than respectful attention, the project member will go on to solve his problem in the middle of his presentation.

10.9 SUMMARY

The area of motivation concerned with giving the project member the opportunity to provide his own reasons for doing his task assignments, making your expectations clear, giving credit, providing timely constructive criticism, and submitting honest performance appraisals requires skill development. However, if you carry out your project leader responsibilities, you've taken a large step toward providing an environment condusive to performance. Such project leader responsibilities are

1. Encouraging your project members to coordinate their activities with one another, which will contribute to the formation of a team.
2. Keeping down contingencies, which will create working conditions condusive to performance.
3. Carrying out your coordination and communication responsibilities, which will contribute to performance by making goals clear.

A. REQUEST
FOR CHANGE FORM

Once the functional specifications for a system have been frozen, any user-originated requests for change of the definition of the system must be made on a *request for change form* (see Figure A-1), and must adhere to the following procedure.

The request for change form is initiated by the user. It's then submitted to the project leader, who acknowledges the receipt of, and files for future action, all postponable changes. For changes requiring immediate action, the project leader spells out the impact of the change on the system and the project, and then estimates the change in schedule and budget required to institute the change in specifications. This information is transmitted to the user. When the user approves the changes in schedule and budget, the specifications change is implemented.

The request for change form, a four-part form, is completed as follows:

1. The requesting department is identified.
2. The project is identified by project number.
3. The requested change is described.
4. The benefits to be derived from the change are listed.
5. The change is classified as
   a. Immediate—A change that must be immediately incorporated into the design.
   b. Postponable—A change that's desirable but which can wait for implementation until the initial system is accepted.
6. The form is approved by the requesting department head.
7. The original and two copies are submitted to the system development department.
8. If the change is classified as postponable, the project leader acknowledges the request by signing the form and returns the copies to the user.
9. If the change is classified as immediate:
   a. The project leader spells out the impact of the change. This description includes:
      i) The new tasks that must be set up to effect the change and the person hours required to complete these tasks.
      ii) The increase in person hours required for each already existing task.
   b. The estimated change in schedule is entered.
   c. The estimated change in budget is entered.
   d. The project leader signs the form.
   e. The original and one copy are returned to the user.
   f. If the user accepts the schedule and budget changes, the form is approved by the requesting department head.
   g. The original is submitted to the system development department.
   h. The change is implemented.

REQUEST FOR CHANGE FORM

REQUESTING DEPT.	PROJECT NO.
PROJECT NAME	

DESCRIPTION OF CHANGE

BENEFITS

☐ IMMEDIATE	☐ POSTPONABLE

DEPARTMENT HEAD	DATE

IMPACT

DELAY IN SCHEDULE (IN WEEKS)	BUDGET INCREASE (IN DOLLARS)
PROJECT LEADER	DATE
DEPARTMENT HEAD	DATE

ADD PAGES TO FORM AS REQUIRED

Figure A-1. Request for change form.

B. PAYROLL APPLICATION CASE STUDY

I. Introduction

The Omega Corporation is a nationwide service organization consisting of several companies. Each company is organized into regions, the regions are divided into offices, and offices into facilities. All employees are salaried, and transfer between facilities, offices, regions and companies is common.

Over the years, both the corporation's business and organization have expanded to the point where the current payroll system no longer has the ability to reflect the levels of organization in the present corporate structure, transfers within the organization are difficult to handle, and there are many local tax situations that must be handled outside the system. For these reasons, the corporation has decided to redesign its payroll system. The following is a description of the proposed payroll system.

II. Overview

A. Purpose

The payroll system provides the corporate payroll department with an automated system which

1. Provides prompt and accurate payroll checks.
2. Develops and maintains records of employee earnings and deductions.
3. Records and reports various taxes and other statistical data as required by governmental agencies.
4. Produces other payroll-related management information.

B. Features

The system has the following features:

1. A Company, Region, Office, Facility (CROF) code structure is incorporated that allows additions of companies, regions, offices, and facilities as easily as new employees.
2. Selective processing permits the user to process some CROF's and not others.

C. Procedures

The system is divided into four phases. The first three form the backbone of the system and must be run each payroll cycle—that is, twice each month. The fourth

163

phase contains programs which produce quarterly, annual, and supplemental payroll-related management information. Implementation of phase IV isn't part of the current project and isn't described here.

In phase I the old master file, which contains historical payroll data for each employee, is read. Each employee is represented on the file by one record for each company for which he worked during the year. The records on the old master file are updated with data from records on the transaction file. The transaction file includes personal action data, payroll action data, and header record data.

A transaction trail file of all updating actions which have been made to the master file is produced. It's edited and printed in phase III. In addition, all transaction input data is validated and a list of diagnostics is produced. Accompanying the diagnostics is an analysis indicating which CROF locations have been processed.

The input to phase II is the updated old master file created in phase I. Detail calculations are made. Current deductions, such as federal income tax and FICA, and gross pay are calculated. Net pay and current vacation status are also calculated. Year-to-date fields are revised to reflect the new calculations. The processed records are written on an intermediate output file.

The intermediate file is then read and copied onto the new master file. Current and year-to-date information is summarized to the CROF level, and summary records are written on the new master file for each CROF break.

In phase III, the new master file is read and the cyclical reports and checks are produced according to the options available to the payroll department. These options allow selection of reports and the inclusion or exclusion of given CROF codes. Reports such as the payroll deduction register and checks are required for each payroll cycle. Other reports, such as the vacation register and the FICA report, are required only once a month.

The new master file becomes the old master file when all the desired reports have been produced and is retained for input to phase I of the next payroll cycle.

III. System Flowchart

A system flowchart for the proposed payroll system is appended.

IV. Program Specifications

A. Run One: Update

1. Purpose

This program has three functions:

a. Validate the transactions, produce a listing of transactions that contain errors or possible errors with appropriate diagnostics for each transaction listed, and reformat valid transactions.

b. At each payroll cycle, all current fields are reset to zero. At the beginning of each quarter, quarter-to-date fields are reset to zero. At the beginning of each year, year-to-date fields are reset to zero.

c. Update the master file with transactions for new employees and changes for current employees. Processing is selective, based on location request records.

2. Procedures

The transaction file is read and validated.

The location request records are read, edited, and stored internally in a table of requested location codes. Then an analysis of these records is produced, and the run continues.

The two input files, the transaction file and the old master file, are read, and the master file is reset and updated. The updated master, the transaction trail file, and a list of diagnostics is produced.

File control is the most difficult part of this program, for only locations requested by location request records are processed. The CROF code on the master file is used for this selection.

3. Input

a. Old Master

Three types of records exist on the old master file—header records, detail records, and summary records. All records contain 1600 bytes, but they have different content. All header records have employee number 00000. Detail records have employee numbers in the range 00001 through 99997. These records are the ones which are reset and updated.

Two types of summary records can exist on the file. Employee number 99998 is a mid-month summary, employee number 99999 a month-end summary. When the cycle number is odd, both types of summary records exist. When the cycle number is even, only type 99998 exists. All are passed on to the updated master.

b. Transaction File

Transactions provide the information required to update the old master file. Information regarding new employees and changes with respect to current employees are submitted to the payroll department on personnel action forms. These forms are edited by a payroll clerk and submitted to data entry for keying. Errors introduced by overpayment, underpayment, deduction problems, etc., are corrected by means of input keyed from payroll action forms. Values on the forms can be positive or negative depending on the error being corrected.

Three kinds of records may appear on the transaction file and are discussed below:

(i) ID and Date Record—Only one such record exists. It contains the number of the payroll cycle being processed in format YNN, where Y is the year and NN the cycle number.

(ii) Facility Header Records—These records supply titles, addresses, tax information, and work hours in each month for all companies, regions, offices, and facilities.

(iii) Personnel and Payroll Actions—Personnel and payroll actions appear on the file when new employees are added to the master file and when a change is made to a current employee on the master file. Personnel and payroll actions are divided into four types—new employee, personnel data changes, current payroll, and year-to-date payroll.

4. Output
   a. Updated Master
      The updated master contains all the records of the old master in updated form plus records for new employees for whom the required transactions have been entered. Records whose CROF were not to be processed, as indicated by the location request cards, haven't had their cycle numbers updated.
   b. Transaction Trail File
      The transaction trail file contains at least one record for each transaction that's input to the program except for header transactions. Each record contains the new data input to the system for an employee and, for personnel actions, contains the replaced data or a comment. For each transfer, there are two records on the file—one for the CROF where the employee transferred from and one for the CROF where the employee transferred to.
   c. Diagnostics
B. Run Two: Calculate
   1. Purpose
      This program has two functions—detail calculate and summary calculate, as described below.
      a. Detail Calculate—The program calculates current pay and deductions data for each employee. The calculations are based on the payroll cycle, the codes pertaining to the individual, and the adjustments to pay and deductions which are supplied through the update program. The results of the current calculations are reflected across quarter-to-date and year-to-date fields.
      b. Summary Calculate—The program summarizes pay and deduction data calculated in the detail calculate, and produces summary records for each CROF break. The first summary record is a summary of data for the current payroll period, and the second summary record is a summary of the current plus the preceding payroll period, which is produced at month-end only.
   2. Procedures
      a. Detail Calculate
         The program uses subroutines to calculate gross pay, deductions, and net pay. The main program opens the files, reads and selects records to be processed, links to the proper subroutines, updates quarter-to-date and year-to-date fields, and writes the record on an intermediate file.
      b. Summary Calculate
         The program opens the intermediate file and reads records. It copies all header records and detail records onto the new master file and summarizes these detail records. When a header or a summary record is found, a current period summary record is written. The second summary record is created by adding the data from the current summary record to that of the summary record just read. This addition creates a record which contains summary data for the current period plus the previous period.

C. Run Three: Sort Transaction Trail

A standard sort package is used.

D. Run Four: Print Transaction Trail

This program prints a trail of all transactions against the payroll master file for the inspection of the office and facility managers concerned. The program edits all data and shows replacing and replaced data, and comments where appropriate.

E. Run Five: Vacation Report

1. Purpose

The vacation report provides the payroll department and the office managers with a breakdown of vacation pay and accrued vacation hours for each employee, and a summary of this information for each facility.

2. Procedures

The master file is passed, and records which contain vacation information are printed. The vacation information is summarized and, when CROF breaks occur, is printed. Duplicate summaries are suppressed.

F. Run Six: FICA Report

1. Purpose

This run produces the FICA withholding report for the use of the payroll department.

2. Procedures

The master file is passed, and records which contain FICA information are printed. The FICA information is summarized and, when CROF breaks occur, is printed. Duplicate summaries are suppressed.

G. Run Seven: State Unemployment and Disability Report

The purpose of the state unemployment and disability report program is to print the unemployment and disability tax report for states that require them.

H. Run Eight: Produce Reports and Checks Monitor

1. Purpose

This program controls subroutines which produce the checks, payroll deduction register, and master print, and determines which CROF's on the master file these subroutines may use.

2. Procedures

The program reads and validates a report request record and location request records. Errors in these records are indicated, and provision is made for resubmitting these records when errors occur. One pass of the master file is required for each report. The ID and date record is obtained from the header.

Every record on the master file is read and its cycle number checked against that of the ID and date record. Records whose cycle numbers disagree with the ID and date record are bypassed. Valid records are passed to the appropriate subroutine.

When all reports are produced, additional reports can be requested.

3. Subroutine Description

a. Master Print

(i) Purpose

The master print subroutine is an edited dump of the payroll master file and provides the accounting department with a picture of the file contents.

(ii) Procedures

The subroutine receives a record from the payroll master file via the main program, identifies its type, and prints the information in the record in the appropriate format. When the record has been processed, control returns to the main program.

b. Payroll Deduction Register

(i) Purpose

The payroll deduction register provides the accounting department with a record of the checks which have been issued and year-to-date accumulations of payments and deductions.

(ii) Procedures

The subroutine receives a record from the payroll master file via the main program and identifies the type. When a record has been processed, control is returned to the main program.

c. Checks

The subroutine produces the payroll checks for the corporation. The input record is processed if it will produce a meaningful check, and control is returned to the main program.

I. Run Nine: 941 Forms

1. Purpose

This program produces the 941 forms that are sent to the federal government.

2. Procedures

The master file is passed and federal withholding information is extracted from the detail records and printed on the 941 forms. Totals are kept at grand, company, and office levels, and are printed when breaks are encountered in these keys.

J. Run Ten: CROF Code Change

The program changes CROF codes on the master file from a given code to another given code. The program is used to reflect organizational changes and to allow realignment of geographical boundaries. Changes are entered by control cards.

K. Run 11: Sort Old Master

This program is run only when run 10, CROF Code Change, is run. A standard sort is used.

V. Available Personnel

The following is a description of the people with which the project can be staffed.

A. Henry Miller

Rank: Analyst

Age: 26

Education: BA, Mathematics

Experience: Mr. Miller's first commercial experience was with Omega. He has been with the company for four years. His experience has been in commercial applications, where he has worked in such areas as material accounting and land management. He has no previous experience on payroll applications, but in the last few months he has been working with the present payroll system to get as much as possible of what was necessary out of it. In this work he has been consulted from time to time on the design of the new system. Although he has been studying the computer on which the new system is to be built, he has no experience with it. He has three years of COBOL programming experience.

B. Morgan Fried

Rank: Senior Programmer

Age: 31

Education: BA, Education

Experience: Mr. Fried taught public school for six years. He then worked for an insurance company for two years, where he got his first experience with computers. He then joined Omega and has now been with the company for two years. During this time his work has been in the area of commercial applications handling large files on large scale equipment. He has no previous experience on payroll. He has no experience with the computer on which the new payroll is to be installed. He has a half year's experience in COBOL.

C. John Nazarevitz

Rank: Senior Programmer

Age: 28

Education: BA, Speech; Masters, Speech

Experience: Mr. Nazarevitz did some programming in the scientific and statistics areas while in school. His first commercial experience was with Omega. He has been with the company for two years. During this time he has worked on commercial applications, mostly programs that perform some type of calculation or summary operation. He has no previous experience with payroll or the computer to be used with the new payroll. He has one half year's experience with COBOL.

D. Charlene Long

Rank: Programmer

Age: 23

Education: BA, English

Experience: After graduating from college, Ms. Long worked for a bank for two years, where she learned to program. Before leaving the bank, she spent a short period of time working on the bank payroll. She then joined Omega, where she has been for the last month. During this time she has been training herself by reading manuals on the computer on which the new payroll is to be installed. She has no COBOL experience.

E. William Kramer

Rank: Programmer

Age: 23

Education: High School Graduate

Experience: After graduating from high school, Mr. Kramer spent four years in the Air Force, during the last three years of which he was a programmer in the inventory control area. He has recently been discharged and is a new hire at Omega. He has no experience in payroll or with the computer to be used with the new payroll system. He has three years of COBOL experience.

F. Norman Nickelson

Rank: Programmer

Age: 23

Education: BA, Mathematics

Experience: After college, Mr. Nickelson joined Omega, where he has been now for two years. He has done some commercial work, but most of his time has been spent in the area of statistics. He has no experience in payroll. He has a year's experience with the computer on which the payroll will be installed. He has no COBOL experience.

G. Eva Catalfo

Rank: Programmer

Age: 24

Education: BA, Chemistry

Experience: After graduating from college, Ms. Catalfo spent three years working as a laboratory technician. During this time she took a home study course and an evening school course on programming, on both of which she did well. She's a new hire at Omega. Both of her courses have included COBOL and, in the evening school course, she had limited exposure to the computer on which the payroll will be installed.

H. Jules Tabbert

Rank: Programmer

Age: 21

Education: BA, Computer Science

Experience: Mr. Tabbert recently joined Omega after graduation. His overall grade average, as well as his computer science grade average, was C+. He has taken a one semester course in COBOL, and the computer on which he worked at school is the same as the one on which the payroll is to be implemented.

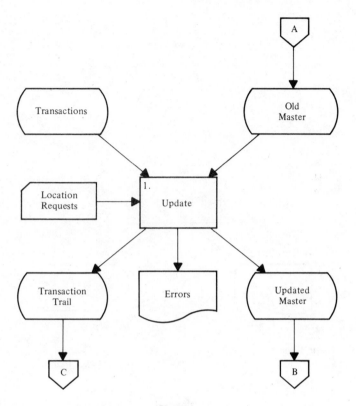

Phase I

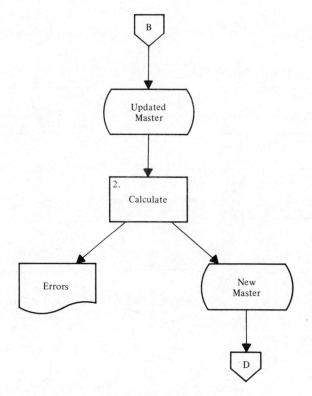

Phase II

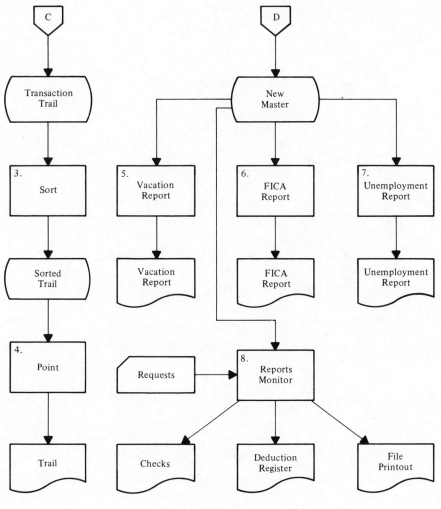

Phase III

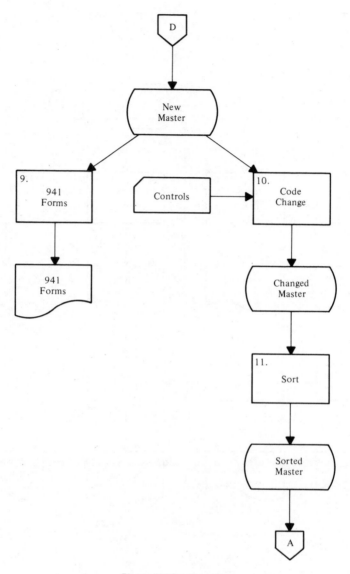

Phase III (*Continued*)

C. BUBBLE CHART

Functional and design specifications for the payroll system described in Appendix B have been frozen. Development of the system is about to enter the construction phase. We're now going to develop a plan for the construction phase. The project is to take the system from its present design state to the point where the payroll department begins to use the system to generate the company's paychecks and maintain its payroll records.

The functional specifications specify that the system acceptance test will consist of running the new payroll system in parallel with the old system for four payroll cycles. The payroll system cycles twice a month. Therefore, we must process two months of payroll data in parallel. It's not necessary to conduct this parallel operation in real time— that is, we may save up data from previous payroll cycles and then cycle the new system as frequently as we think we can to produce and check the parallel results.

We're now going to take the first steps in developing the plan for the construction phase. Specifically, we're to develop

a. A list of the tasks to be performed in the construction phase.
b. A bubble chart showing the dependencies between these tasks.

In developing our task list, we consider activities only. We don't concern ourselves with the functions performed by the system.

Also, we develop our task list at a high level. For example, there are 11 programs in the payroll system. We consider the development of these programs—specification, structure, coding, development of unit test data, and unit test—as just one task in our task list.

A bubble chart showing the dependency between the tasks making up the construction phase of the payroll system project is shown in Figure C-1. Some remarks concerning this bubble chart are

a. The bubble chart is a high level chart. The bubbles represent groups of tasks. If the chart were constructed on the basis of a finer task distinction, a more intricate network of dependencies would be revealed. The point we're emphasizing by developing the bubble chart at this level is that there are many tasks other than developing programs which must be done to make the system operational.
b. There's nothing immutable about all the dependencies shown in this bubble chart. For example, if we decided to use the file conversion procedures to develop unit test data, then program development is dependent on the development of these conversion procedures.
c. However, some dependencies on this bubble chart are necessary. For example
1) Programs must be developed before preparation of the operations manual can be finished. Until program development is complete, there's always the possibility

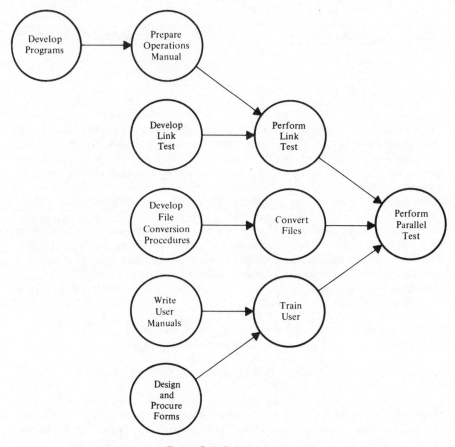

Figure C-1. Bubble chart.

that some change in program construction will have ramifications as far as operations are concerned.

2) The link test can't be complete until it has been demonstrated that the computer center can run the system in its normal operations environment. Therefore, the operations manual must be prepared before link testing can be completed.

3) The link test must be developed before it can be performed.

D. PROGRAM SPECIFICATION

VALIDATION MODULE OF RUN 1, THE UPDATE PROGRAM

Purpose

The purpose of the validation module is to validate all transaction input to the payroll system and produce

I. A listing of transactions that contain errors or possible errors with appropriate diagnostics for each transaction listed.
II. Reformatted valid transactions that are passed to the reset and update module of the update program.

Input

I. Transactions provide the information required to update the payroll master file.
   A. Information regarding new employees or changes with respect to current employees is submitted to the payroll department on personnel action forms. These forms are edited by a payroll clerk and submitted to data entry for keying.
   B. Errors introduced by overpayment, underpayment, deduction problems, etc., are corrected by means of input keyed from payroll action forms. Numeric values on the forms can be positive or negative depending on the cause of the original error.
II. All input transactions are combined into a single transaction file, which is input to the validation module. Transaction types appearing on the transaction file and the format of these transaction types are given below.

   A. ID and Date Record

Column	Information
2-8	'PAYROLL'
21-26	End of the pay period in MMDDYY format
36-53	The date the payroll is being run—example: July 24, 1967
54-59	Date to appear on checks in MMDDYY format.
61-65	'CYCLE'
67-69	Three digit cycle number. The first digit of the cycle number is the last digit of the current year. The next two digits of the cycle number are the chronological number of the payroll being run this

year—for example: the fifth payroll cycle of 1985 would be cycle 505.

B. Facility Header Records
   1. Common information.

Column	Information
1–5	'00000'
6–13	CROF
21–26	Effective date in MMDDYY format.
80	'A'

   2. Variable Information

Record Type	Position	Information
1	20	'1'
	36–75	Company name
2	20	'2'
	36–75	Region name
3	20	'3'
	36–75	Office name
4	20	'4'
	36–75	Facility name
5	20	'5'
	36–75	Mailing name
6	20	'6'
	36–75	Second line of mailing address
7	20	'7'
	36–75	Third line of mailing address.
8	20	'8'
	36,37	Unemployment code
	38–42	Unemployment rate—example: 2.2% would be 00220
	43,44	Disability code
	45–49	Less than five years vacation hours—example: 10.00 hours would be 01000
	50–54	Greater than five years vacation hours—example: 13.33 hours would be 01333
	55–61	Work hours in year—example: 2080 hours would be 0208000
	62–66	Work hours in January including holidays—example: 176 hours would be 17600
9	20	'9'
	36–40	Work hours in February including holidays
	41–45	Work hours in March
	46–50	Work hours in April
	51–55	Work hours in May
	56–60	Work hours in June
	61–65	Work hours in July

	66–70	Work hours in August
	71–75	Work hours in September
A	20	'A'
	36–40	Work hours in October
	41–45	Work hours in November
	46–50	Work hours in December

C. Personnel and Payroll Action Records

Position	Information
1–5	Employee number
6–13	CROF
14	Transaction type
15–20	Effective date in MMDDYY format
21–29	First nine characters of name with last name first
30–33	Form number
34,35	Record number
36–75	Input data—information and format are shown on the personnel and payroll action forms
80	'B'

III. The only sequence restriction imposed on the input records is that the ID and date record must be the first record on the file.

Output

I. Diagnostics Listing
Information concerning transactions that contain errors or possible errors are printed on the diagnostics listing. This information consists of
A. A formatted image of the transaction involved.
B. Diagnostic messages. The content of specific diagnostic messages is given in the procedure section of this specification.

II. Reformatted Valid Transactions
A. Record length: 80 characters
B. Sequence: Same as for the input transaction file
C. Format
1. The format of the ID and date record isn't changed.
2. The format of facility header records isn't changed.
3. The first 35 positions of personnel and payroll action records are reformatted as follows:

Position on Output	Position on Input
1–14	1–14
15,16	34,35
17–20	30–33
21–26	15–20
27–35	21–29
36–80	36–80

Procedure

I. ID and Date Record
   A. The first record read must be an ID and date record. It's validated as follows:
      1. Positions 2–8 must be 'PAYROLL'.
      2. Positions 68–69 must be between '00' and '25'.
      3. If positions 68–69 equal '01' and
         a. Position 26 is not = '9', position 67 must be 1 greater than position 26.
         b. Position 26 '9', position 67 must be zero.
      4. If positions 68–69 are not = '01', position 67 must be equal to position 26.
      5. Positions 54–59 must be a valid date.
      6. Positions 36–53 must not be blank.
      7. Positions 21–26 must be a valid date.
   B. When errors are found on the ID and date record, a message is displayed identifying the error and requesting a corrected ID and date record.
   C. When a valid ID and date record has been read
      1. The following information is saved:
         a. Cycle number, positions 67–69.
         b. End of pay period, positions 21–26.
      2. The ID and date record is passed to the reset and update module.
II. Validation of Transactions
   When validity errors occur, the record is printed and all diagnostics pertaining to the record are printed afterward. There are two types of diagnostics: fatal and warning. If a record contains an error that produces a fatal diagnostic, the record isn't written on the intermediate output file. All other records are written on the intermediate output file.

   A. If position 80 contains an 'A', the record is a facility header and is validated as follows:
      1. Positions 1–5 must contain '00000'.
         Diagnostic: **FATAL FACILITY HEADER MUST HAVE EMPLOYEE NUMBER 00000
      2. Positions 6–13 must be numeric.
         Diagnostic: **FATAL NONNUMERIC CROF CODE
      3. Position 20 must be '1–9' or 'A'.
         Diagnostic: **FATAL INVALID HEADER CODE
      4. If the header code (position 20) is
         a. '1'–'7', positions 36–75 shouldn't be blank.
            Diagnostic: WARNING NO TITLE ON THIS FACILITY HEADER
         b. '8', positions 36–75 must not all be blank, but individual fields may be blank. Each field that isn't blank must be numeric. Other validation is listed below.
            (1) Tax code (positions 36,37) must be less than '57'.
                Diagnostic: **FATAL INVALID LOCAL UNEMPLOYMENT CODE

(2) Local unemployment rate (positions 38–42) must be greater than 0.09 and less than 10.01.
Diagnostic: **FATAL LOCAL UNEMPLOYMENT RATE INVALID

(3) Local disability code (positions 43,44) must be less than '57'.
Diagnostic: **FATAL LOCAL DISABILITY CODE INVALID

(4) Less than five years vacation hours (positions 45–49) must be greater than 7.99 and less than 20.01.
Diagnostic: **FATAL INVALID LESS THAN 5 YEARS VACATION HOURS

(5) Greater than five years vacation hours (positions 50–54) must be greater than 7.99 and less than 20.01.
Diagnostic: **FATAL INVALID GREATER THAN 5 YEARS VACATION HOURS

(6) Work hours in year (positions 55–61) must be 1885 or 2080.
Diagnostic: **FATAL INVALID WORK HOURS IN YEAR

(7) Base hours in month (positions 62–66) must be greater than 99 and less than 201.
Diagnostic: **FATAL INVALID BASE HOURS IN MONTH

c. '9', positions 36–75 must be numeric.
Diagnostic: **FATAL INVALID BASE HOURS IN MONTH

d. 'A', positions 36–50 must be numeric.
Diagnostic: **FATAL INVALID BASE HOURS IN MONTH

B. If position 80 contains a 'B', the record is a payroll or personnel action.

1. General validation for all records in this group is

a. Employee number (positions 1–5) must be in the range '00001'–'99997'.
Diagnostic: **FATAL INVALID EMPLOYEE NUMBER

b. CROF code (columns 6–13) must be numeric.
Diagnostic: **FATAL NONNUMERIC CROF CODE

c. Transaction number (positions 14–16) must be within one of the following ranges:
(1) '001'–'015'.
(2) '101'–'115'.
(3) '201'–'230'.
(4) '301'–'327'.
Diagnostic: **FATAL ILLEGAL TRANSACTION NUMBER

d. Form number (positions 17–20) shouldn't be blank.
Diagnostic: WARNING NO FORM NUMBER

e. Effective date (positions 21–16) must be
(1) A valid date in the form MMDDYY.
Diagnostic: **FATAL INVALID EFFECTIVE DATE
(2) Equal to or earlier than the stored date from the ID and date record.
Diagnostic: **FATAL EFFECTIVE DATE PUTS TRANSACTION IN LATER PAY PERIOD

2. Specific validation for input data is done by form type as well as record type.

If the form

a. Is a personnel action (position 14 is '0' or '1'), and the record type (positions 15,16) is

   (1) '01', the record is for assignment or transfer

      (a) Positions 36–43 must be numeric.

         Diagnostic: **FATAL ASSIGNMENT OF CROF CODE NOT COMPLETE

      (b) If the employee is new (position 14 is 'C'), position 36–43 must equal positions 6–13.

         Diagnostic: **FATAL FOR NEW EMPLOYEE POSITIONS 6–13 AND 36–43 MUST BE EQUAL.

   (2) '02', the record is for name and marital status

      (a) Positions 36–65 must not be blank.

         Diagnostic: **FATAL NO NAME GIVEN

      (b) Position 66 should be 'M' or 'S'. If it's neither, move 'S' to position 66.

         Diagnostic: WARNING .ILLEGAL MARITAL STATUS, ASSUME SINGLE

      (c) There must be one and only one comma in positions 36–65.

         Diagnostic: **FATAL THERE MUST BE ONE AND ONLY ONE COMMA IN NAME

   (3) '03' or '04', the record is for address

      (a) Positions 36–65 shouldn't be blank.

         Diagnostic: WARNING NO ADDRESS GIVEN

      (b) Position 71 must be 'M', 'L' or 'B'. If not, move 'L' to position 71.

         Diagnostic: WARNING CANNOT DETERMINE IF MAILING OR LEGAL. ASSUME LEGAL

      (c) If positions 15,16 are '04', positions 66–70 should be numeric.

         Diagnostic: WARNING NO ZIP CODE GIVEN

   (4) '05', the record is for home telephone.

      (a) Positions 36–38 should be numeric.

         Diagnostic: WARNING INVALID AREA CODE GIVEN

      (b) Positions 39–45 must not be blank, and positions 41–45 must be numeric.

         Diagnostic: **FATAL INVALID TELEPHONE NUMBER GIVEN

   (5) '06', the record is for social security number, birth date, and sex.

      (a) Positions 36–44 must be numeric or blank. If not, positions 36–44 are blanked.

         Diagnostic: WARNING SOCIAL SECURITY NUMBER IS ILLEGAL, NONE USED

      (b) Birth date (positions 45–50) should be a valid date in the form MMDDYY or blank. If not, blank positions 45–50.

         Diagnostic: WARNING DATE IS BAD, NONE USED

      (c) If the record is for a new employee (position 14 is '0'), position

51 must be '*M*' or '*F*'. If the record is a change (position 14 is '1'), position 51 must be '*M*', '*F*', or blank.

Diagnostic: **FATAL CANNOT DETERMINE SEX

(6) '07', the record is for status and salary.

    (a) Position 51 must be '*F*', '*P*', or blank.

    Diagnostic: **FATAL CANNOT DETERMINE STATUS

    (b) If position 51 is '*F*', positions 52–55 must be numeric, and positions 56–59 must be blank. If position 51 is '*P*', positions 56–59 must be blank. If position 51 is blank, either positions 52–55 must be numeric and positions 56–59 must be blank, or positions 56–59 must be numeric and positions 52–55 must be blank.

    Diagnostic: **FATAL SALARY IS INCORRECT

    (c) If position 51 is blank, positions 52–55 are numeric, and positions 56–59 are blank, move '*F*' to column 51.

    (d) If position 51 is blank, positions 56–59 are numeric, and positions 52–55 are blank, move '*P*' to position 51.

(7) '08', the record is for rank and title.

    (a) Positions 38,39 must not be blank.

    Diagnostic: **FATAL NO RANK ASSIGNED

    (b) Positions 40–54 shouldn't be blank.

    Diagnostic: WARNING NO TITLE GIVEN

(8) '09', the record is for hospital coverage.

    (a) Position 36 must be blank or contain 'Y', 'N', or zero.

    Diagnostic: **FATAL INVALID LIFE INSURANCE CODE

    (b) Position 37 must be blank or a number less than '5'.

    Diagnostic: **FATAL CANNOT DETERMINE TYPE OF HOSPITAL COVERAGE

    (c) Positions 38–41 must contain a date

      aa. In the form MMDDYY.

      bb. For the current month or the following month. If the date is further in advance, the following diagnostic appears:

      **FATAL HOSPITALIZATION SCHEDULED TO START MORE THAN 1 MONTH IN ADVANCE

      If the date is prior to the current month, the following diagnostic appears:

      WARNING HOSPITALIZATION WILL START THIS MONTH

(9) '10', the record is for federal tax.

    (a) Positions 38,39 must be blank or numeric.

    Diagnostic: **FATAL INVALID EXEMPTIONS

    (b) If positions 38,39 are numeric, they should be less than '13'.

    Diagnostic: WARNING QUESTIONABLE EXEMPTIONS

    (c) Positions 43–48 should be blank or a positive number. If not, move zero to positions 43–48.

    Diagnostic: WARNING INVALID ADDITIONAL WITHHOLDING, ZERO USED

     (d) If positions 43–48 are numeric, they should be less than $100.00.
        Diagnostic: WARNING QUESTIONABLE ADDITIONAL WITHHOLDING

(10) '11', the record is for state tax.

     (a) Positions 36,37 must be blank or numeric.
        Diagnostic: **FATAL ILLEGAL TAX CODE

     (b) Positions 38,39 must be blank or numeric, or position 38 must be '*M*' or '*S*', and position 39 a number.
        Diagnostic: **FATAL INVALID EXEMPTIONS

     (c) If positions 38,39 are numeric, they should be less than '12'.
        Diagnostic: WARNING QUESTIONABLE EXEMPTIONS

     (d) Positions 40–42 should be blank or numeric and in the range between zero and 1.00. If not, set positions 40–42 to 1.00.
        Diagnostic: WARNING BAD PERCENTAGE, 100 PERCENT USED

     (e) Positions 43–48 are validated as in (9) (c) and (d).

(11) '12', the record is for city tax. All positions are validated as in the state tax records.

(12) '15', the record is for termination.

     (a) If the cycle is month-end (odd) or position 51 is '*Y*', the following fields are made zero:
        aa. Regular hours (positions 41–45).
        bb. Overtime hours (positions 36–40).
        cc. Vacation hours taken (positions 46–50).

     (b) If the cycle is mid-month (even) and position 51 isn't '*Y*'
        aa. Positions 36–40 should be a positive number. If they aren't, make this field zero.
        Diagnostic: WARNING INVALID OVERTIME HOURS, ASSUME ZERO
        bb. Positions 41–45 must be a positive number.
        Diagnostic: **FATAL NEED TO KNOW HOURS WORKED UNTIL TERMINATION
        cc. Positions 46–50 should be a positive number. If they aren't, make them zero.
        Diagnostic: WARNING INVALID VACATION HOURS TAKEN, WILL ASSUME NO VACATION USED

     (c) Position 51 should be '*Y*' or '*N*'. If not, make it an '*N*'.
        Diagnostic: WARNING MANUAL CHECK INDICATOR IS INVALID, WILL ASSUME NO MANUAL CHECK WRITTEN

(13) None of the above.
     Diagnostic: **FATAL NO CODING HAS BEEN IMPLEMENTED FOR THIS TYPE OF TRANSACTION

b. A current payroll action (position 14 is '2') and the record type (positions 15,16) is

     (1) '01'–'10', '18'–'28' or '30', positions 36–42 must be numeric.
        Diagnostic: **FATAL NONNUMERIC VALUE IN NUMERIC FIELD

    (2) '11'-'17'

        (a) Positions 36–42 must be numeric and positions 43–49 must be blank, positions 36–42 must be blank and positions 43–49 must be numeric, or positions 36–42 and positions 43–49 must both be numeric.

            Diagnostic: **FATAL NONNUMERIC VALUE IN NUMERIC FIELD

        (b) If positions 36–42 are numeric and positions 43–49 are blank, move zeros to positions 43–49.

        (c) If positions 36–42 are blank and positions 43–49 are numeric, move zeros to positions 36–42.

    (3) '29', positions 36–41 must contain a valid date in MMDDYY format.

        Diagnostic: **FATAL INVALID LAST DAY OF LEAVE

  c. A year-to-date payroll action (position 14 is '3') and the record type (positions 15,16) is

    (1) '01'-'26', the record is validated the same way as is a current payroll action.

    (2) '27'

        (a) Positions 36,37 must be in the range '01'-'06'.

            Diagnostic: **FATAL INVALID TAX TYPE

        (b) Positions 38,39 must be numeric.

            Diagnostic: **FATAL INVALID TAX CODE

        (c) Positions 40–60 must not be completely blank.

            Diagnostic: **FATAL INVALID ADJUSTMENT

        (d) Gross (positions 40–46) must be blank or numeric.

            Diagnostic: **FATAL NONNUMERIC GROSS

        (e) If positions 40–46 are blank, move zeros to positions 40–46.

        (f) Taxable gross (positions 47–53) must be blank or numeric.

            Diagnostic: **FATAL NONNUMERIC TAXABLE GROSS

        (g) If columns 47–53 are blank, move zeros to columns 47–53.

        (h) Withholding (positions 54–60) must be blank or numeric.

            Diagnostic: **FATAL NONNUMERIC WITHHOLDING

        (i) If columns 54–60 are blank, move zeros to columns 54–60.

C. None of the above

    Diagnostic: **FATAL THIS RECORD INVALID OR OUT OF SEQUENCE

III. Controls

At the end of module execution, the following are printed on the diagnostics listing:

A. Number of fatal diagnostics.

B. Number of records dropped.

C. Number of warning diagnostics on records that were dropped.

D. Number of warning diagnostics on records that weren't dropped.

E. Number of records read.

F. Number of records written.

E. TIME ESTIMATE

Run 1, the update program of the payroll system described in Appendix B, has been designed in such a way that it's made up of two modules—a validation module and a reset and update module. Program specifications for the validation module are given in Appendix D. John Nazarevitz has been assigned the responsibility for developing this module. The program is to be written in COBOL. All coding for this module is to be developed from scratch. We use the algorithm for estimating program development time,as given in Chapter 5, to estimate the number of person-days it will take Nazarevitz to develop this program. This algorithm generates an estimate that includes the time to write program specifications. In the case at hand, these specifications have already been written, and we adjust the result we get from the algorithm accordingly.

According to the program development time estimating algorithm, the estimate of the time Nazarevitz needs to develop the validation module is constructed by following a series of steps. The first step is to determine module complexity. This step is subdivided into two parts—weighting the module's input and output, and weighting the module's processing functions.

We weight the module's input and output by counting them.

a. Input transaction file.
b. Output:

   1) Diagnostics listing.
   2) Reformated valid transactions.

Thus, the input output weight is three.

We weight the processing functions by using the table in the text.

a. Data Rearrangement—A minimum is called for by the module specification. The most we can weight this function is one for simple.
b. Decisions—By themselves, the decisions in the module aren't complex. But there are a lot of them. Therefore, we must weight this function at least complex. Let's assign it a weight of four.
c. Calculation—This function is also minimal. A weight of one for simple is the most we can assign.

Thus, total program complexity weight for the module is:

Input output	3
Data rearrangement	1
Decisions	4
Calculation	1
Total	9

All code is to be developed from scratch, so the module's complexity weight isn't adjusted for adaptability.

The second step in estimating how long it will take Nazarevitz to develop the validation module is to determine his programmer capability. This step is also divided into two parts—weighting Nazarevitz's general programming skill and weighting the relation between his application knowledge and the application knowledge needed to develop the module.

With respect to Nazarevitz's general programming skill, he has been working on commercial applications for two years. It would seem fair to assume that he knows what a validation program is and how it should be structured. He has a half year's experience in COBOL. A weight of 1.5 looks like the maximum appropriate to Nazarevitz's general programming skill. Shading this weight to a lower value might even be more appropriate.

With respect to application knowledge, detailed payroll knowledge isn't necessary to develop the validation module. Consequently, Nazarevitz needs only some payroll knowledge.

Nazarevitz has no detailed knowledge of payroll. However, few people are ignorant of payroll. So let's say Nazarevitz has some knowledge of payroll.

This sets the weight for application knowledge at 0.75. Adding the weights for general programming skill (1.5) and application knowledge (0.75) gives a weight of 2.25 for Nazarevitz's programming capability.

Multiplying the program complexity weight of nine by the programmer capability weight of 2.25 gives an estimate of 20.25 person-days for Nazarevitz to develop the validation module.

Suppose we estimate that it would have taken Nazarevitz three days to develop the program specifications for the validation module. Then the estimate for Nazarevitz to complete development of the module is 17 days.

F. PROJECT PLAN

In Appendix C we developed a bubble chart to show the dependency between the tasks that must be done to take the payroll system described in Appendix B from its present design state to the point where the payroll department begins to use the system to generate the company's paychecks and maintain its payroll records. We're now going to complete the development of the plan for the construction phase of the payroll system project.

This job must be done in 160 working days. That is, 160 working days from now the payroll department must be using the new system to generate the company's paychecks and maintain its payroll records. Consequently, the acceptance test and all other tasks must be completed in 160 working days.

There are 20 working days in a month. Consequently, we have eight months in which to complete this job. If you do a little calculation on the basis of this definition of a working day, you'll soon come to the conclusion that there are 48 weeks in a year. This is, of course, a misrepresentation. But for planning long-term projects, it yields two advantages:

a. It standardizes weeks at five days each and months at four weeks each.
b. It automatically allows four weeks a year for holidays and vacations. As a consequence, we can develop our plan without the need to assign specific calendar days to the time axis of our bar chart.

To develop our plan, we use the task time estimates shown in Figure F-1. This chart is read as follows:

a. People are divided into two groups.
   1) Senior people.
   2) Junior people.
b. Senior people do tasks faster than juniors. For example, it takes a senior person 28 days to prepare program 1 and another 28 days to test it, while it takes a junior 39 days to prepare program 1 and another 39 days to test it.
c. Henry Miller, Morgan Fried, and John Nazarevitz are senior people—all the others are juniors.
d. The third entry isn't for one sort. It's for both sorts—programs 3 and 11.

These estimates pertain only to the develop programs bubble in the bubble chart. We must estimate the time required to do the other tasks on the bubble chart.

Computer unit test turnaround is essentially instantaneous. Blocks of link test computer time can be scheduled when needed. All programs are to be written in COBOL. No unusual delays or interruptions are anticipated.

Our plan is shown in Figure F-2.

Task	Prepare		Test	
	Senior	Junior	Senior	Junior
1. Update	28	39	28	39
2. Calculate	50	60	50	60
3. 11. Both Sorts	2	3	2	3
4. Print Transaction Trail	10	14	10	14
5. Vacation Report	13	18	13	18
6. FICA Report	13	18	13	18
7. Unemployment Report	15	18	15	18
8. Reports Monitor	33	46	33	46
9. 941 Forms	10	14	10	14
10. Code Change	13	18	13	18

Figure F-1 Persondays required per task.

The plan shown in Figure F-2 is only one of many feasible plans. Plan development involves choices among alternatives, and no one set of choices is necessarily right. We tell you why we made the choices we did. The best plan for a given job is one that

a. Meets the requirements of the job and its external restraints.
b. Everyone involved with agrees is reasonable.
c. You feel most comfortable with.

A: Develop Training Program
B: Cobol Training
C: 3.11. Sorts
D: Operations Manual

Figure. F-2 Project plan.

In developing our plan, we adopted the principle of developing a safe plan. Since there's concern with getting the payroll system in and operating smoothly, we wanted a plan that allows us to absorb as many difficulties as possible and still meet our deadline. Thus, if everything goes as planned, we'll have the system built after only two-thirds of the time allocated to system construction has elapsed. The remaining one-third of the time is spent making sure the system hangs together, getting the files converted, and getting the user trained.

We started by deciding to take a full two months to get the files converted and to run the parallel test. Consequently, we blocked off the last eight weeks for this purpose.

The payroll system is a batch system. Consequently, if we do thorough unit testing, link testing shouldn't be too demanding. Moreover, if we test program links as the programs are developed, there should be minimal link testing needed after all the programs have been constructed. Therefore, we allowed only two weeks for link testing, which is blocked off just before entering the file conversion and parallel testing period.

This allowance for link testing, file conversion, and acceptance testing left 22 weeks for constructing the system. Although no unusual delays or interruptions are anticipated, and thus a contingency level of 10% might be reasonable, we decided to follow our conservative bent and allow for a contingency level of about 15%. Consequently, we blocked off the three weeks preceding the system test for contingencies. This left 19 weeks, or 95 days, to devote to individual tasks.

Our next decision was to appoint Miller project leader. We chose Miller because of his seniority at Omega and his experience with the current payroll system.

We then inspected the programs making up the system and determined that programs 1, 2, and 8 are critical. That is, if any of them don't run, the system is down. We decided that, if possible, we'd assign senior people to these programs.

It will take senior personnel 222 person days to develop these programs.

Critical Program	Senior Person Days
1	56
2	100
8	66
	222

If we assign senior people to these programs, we'll need three senior people. But unless we have Miller develop one of these programs, we've only two senior people available, Fried and Nazarevitz. Our inclination was to not use Miller for such tasks, so at this point in plan development, our operating assumption was that a junior person is going to develop one of these programs.

Program 2 involves calculations and summaries, and Nazarevitz has experience with both. Therefore, we assigned him to this program. This assignment cuts Nazarevitz's contingency allowance to two weeks. However, he's a senior person, so we decided to take our chances.

We assigned Fried to program 1.

This task assignment left us with juniors to handle the other program development tasks. These tasks require 298 person-days.

Program	Junior Person-Days
3,11	6
4	28
5	36
6	36
7	36
8	92
9	28
10	<u>36</u>
	298

Dividing the above total by 95 indicated that we must assign at least four juniors to the project.

We were now getting some idea of project size. Consequently, we were ready to make task assignments for the project leader. First, we decided that, during the acceptance test, we'd cut the size of the project to the project leader and the two senior people. This made for a small project during this period. Therefore, we thought Miller might be able to assume responsibility for user training, which would be going on during this period. This meant he'd also have to take responsibility for some user training before entering the acceptance period, and he'd also have to develop the training program, which would consume most of his time during the link test and contingency periods. But we wanted Miller to take the responsibility for the training, so he'd maintain a user attitude toward the system. Therefore, we assigned these training tasks to him.

Our calculations indicated that, during the first five months of the project, there'd be six or seven people on the project. Therefore, we decided not to assign Miller any detailed tasks during this period, since his time is going to be consumed by his project management responsibilities.

Now that we had completed these task assignments, we could see that, in addition to the remaining program development tasks, the tasks of developing the file conversion procedures and the link test, and preparing the operations and user manuals were still unassigned. Consequently, we were going to use all five juniors on the project.

We assigned Nickelson the tasks most directly related to the new computer, because he was the only person with work experience on it. Thus, we had him prepare the operations manual and develop the sorts and file conversion procedures. Because the payroll has previously been automated, file conversion can be accomplished by program; so developing the conversion procedure involves developing a conversion program. Because we thought the conversion program might be useful in generating unit test data, we scheduled it to be completed as soon as possible. Since Nickelson is going to develop the conversion program, we decided to keep him on the project during the week the file is converted. Finally, since Nickelson is a junior, we gave him as much contingency allowance as possible.

Among the juniors, Kramer is both the most experienced programmer and the most experienced COBOL programmer. Thus, we assigned him to program 8. However, Kramer is a new hire. Consequently, we wanted a fallback position. Therefore, we gave Fried a lot of contingency allowance, so he could pitch in and help Kramer if necessary.

Long has some payroll experience. On the theory that programs 6 and 9 were more payroll related than 4, 5, 7, or 10, we assigned Long to programs 6 and 9.

Catalfo seems to be a self-starter; so we assigned her to develop the link test, which we consider critical. This project is going to involve 454 person-days of program development. Using a ratio of eight to one, this means link test development will require 12 person-weeks.

Also because Catalfo is a self-starter, we assigned her to develop the forms. This task shouldn't take long, since most of forms design was completed during functional specification. We scheduled forms development as early as possible, because once specimen forms have been developed and approved by the user, a long lead time is involved in getting printed forms from the supplier.

Finally, since Catalfo is a junior, we gave her as much contingency allowance as possible.

Remembering that Fried was a teacher and might, therefore, be suited to writing the user manual, we assigned him to this task. Since this task is primarily a matter of modifying the functional specifications to convert them into a user manual, we felt five weeks was plenty of time to complete this task.

This left programs 4, 5, 7, and 10. Programs 4, 5, and 7 are report programs; so we assigned them to Tabbert. This left program 10 for Nickelson. Because we felt that programs 4 and 10 were more critical than program 5, we scheduled Tabbert's time such that he'd work on program 5 last. And because we thought program 4 might come in useful during unit testing, we scheduled Tabbert to work on this program first.

Neither Nickelson nor Long had any COBOL background. Consequently, one week each was set aside for their training.

Some people would like to use program 2 to generate test data for programs 4-10. Consequently, they schedule the unit testing of programs 4-10 to take place after development of program 2 is complete. This makes for a tight schedule with exposure to overrun. What should be recognized is that the output of program 2 is the input to program 1. Once we've generated test data for program 1, we have test data for programs 4-10. Thus waiting until program 2 is complete isn't necessary.

G. COST ESTIMATE

In Appendix F we developed a plan to take the payroll system, described in Appendix B, from its present design state to the point where the payroll department begins to use the system to generate the company's paychecks and maintain its payroll records. We now develop a cost estimate for the construction phase of the payroll system project. Personnel costs, including overhead, are $1500 a week for analysts, $1000 a week for senior programmers, and $750 a week for programmers. Computer time cost is 20% of personnel costs. There's no travel requirement, nor are any support services planned. Our cost estimate is shown in the form in Figure G-1.

COST ESTIMATE

PROJECT NO.		PROJECT PHASE *Construction*	
PREPARED BY *Tom Gildersleeve*			DATE

PERSONNEL

NAME	WEEKS	SALARY	COST
Miller	32	$1500	$48,000
Nuzarwitz	32	1000	32,000
Fried	32	1000	32,000
Nickelson	25	750	18,750
Kramer	24	750	18,000
Tabbert	24	750	18,000
Long	18	750	13,500
Catalfo	24	750	18,000
		TOTAL	$198,250

COMPUTER TIME _____ | 39,650 |

TRAVEL AND LIVING EXPENSES _____ | — |

SUPPORT SERVICES | COST

TOTAL	—

GRAND TOTAL | $237,900 |

Figure G-1. Cost estimate.

H. CHECKPOINT PLAN

Normally, project members develop checkpoint plans. However, to be able to evaluate checkpoint plans, you must be able to develop them. In this Appendix, we develop a checkpoint plan designed to monitor the progress of each project member as he works on his tasks to construct the payroll system described in Appendix B. In Appendix F, we developed a plan to take this sytem from its present design state to the point where the payroll department begins to use the system to generate the company's paychecks and maintain its payroll records.

When managing a project, checkpoints for every task performed by a project member are necessary. However, setting up such a checkpoint plan involves redundancy. Consequently, for purposes of this Appendix, we select, from the plan, prototypical tasks and set checkpoints for these tasks only. Consequently, we develop a checkpoint plan for

a. Developing a selected program.
b. Link test development.
c. Link test running.
d. Writing a selected manual.
e. Training program development.

In developing our checkpoint plan, we describe the product or event that signifies attainment of each checkpoint.

Checkpoints for a task must be tied to the delivery of products, whose production is part of doing the task. Since there's no unanimity in the data processing community as to how tasks should be done, there's no possibility of coming up with industry-wide standards for system development task checkpoints. Consequently, the validity of a checkpoint plan depends on the degree to which the checkpoints set up conform to

a. The characteristics of good checkpoints described in chapter 8.
b. The procedure adopted for performing the tasks.

1. Program Development
   We require that a programmer develop a program by following the steps listed below:

   a. First, program specifications are written for the program.
   b. Once the program specifications are complete, the program's logical structure is developed. This structure takes the form of a decision table or some type of flow-chart.
   c. When the logical structure is documented, code is then written.
   d. When coding is complete, a test plan for the program is developed.

e. When the test plan has been developed, unit test data and predetermined results are generated.

f. When the unit test data and predetermined results are ready, unit testing can begin.

Consequently, we propose the following products and events for signifying attainment of checkpoints.

a. The program specifications document.

b. The program structure document.

3. All sheets of coding paper submitted to data entry or all code keyed at the terminal.

d. The test plan document.

e. All unit test data, recorded in the form in which it's going to be used, and all predetermined results documented.

f. Successful running of the program against all unit test data.

For a program with a reasonable development time, we use all six checkpoints. For example, for program 7, which takes 30 days to develop, all six checkpoints are appropriate.

For a program with a short development time, only some of the checkpoints can be used if hassling the programmer is to be avoided. For example, program 4 takes ten days to prepare and another ten days to test. Consequently, for this program, we elect the following four checkpoints:

a. Program specifications.

b. Code.

c. Test plan.

d. Successful test running.

For a program with a long development time, more than six checkpoints are useful. These extra checkpoints are repetitions of the basic six. For example, program 2 has a long development time. Such programs can be logically divided. For example, program 2 has two functions—detail calculate and summary calculate—and can thus be divided into two sections. The two sections can be developed one at a time. The six basic checkpoints can then be applied (all or in part) to each section.

2. Link Test Development

Link test development can be divided into at least three parts:

a. Writing the link test plan.

b. Developing the link test data.

c. Developing the predetermined results.

If this division doesn't produce fine enough tasks, developing the link test data can be divided into at least three parts:

a. Developing test data to see that the system hangs together—that is, that it will run from program 1 through program 11.

    b. Developing data to test normal procedures.

    c. Developing data to test error paths.

3. Link Test Running.

    Link test running can also be divided into at least three parts.

    a. Seeing that the system hangs together.

    b. Testing normal procedures.

    c. Testing error paths.

Link test running can be further divided by adopting the approach of testing subsystems before testing the whole system. For example, programs 1-4 can be link tested in the three phases described above before moving on to the integration of the other programs into the test.

4. Manual Development.

    Products to which checkpoints can be tied for this type of task are

    a. Table of contents.

    b. First draft ready for review.

    c. Final draft.

Production of the first draft can be further divided on the basis of major content areas, such as input and output for the user manual.

5. Training Program Development

    Products to which checkpoints can be tied in this type of task are course outlines, course handouts, student exercises, and solutions to the student exercises.

    Many products produced during system development are documents. To be used as a basis for setting up a checkpoint, a document must be produced as part of accomplishing the task. For example, a status report is a document, but a checkpoint can't be tied to it, because preparation of a status report isn't a part of any system development task.

I. DOCUMENTATION

We've frequently had something to say about documentation in this book. However, our observations have always been in the context of some other subject.

Documentation is an important topic. In this Appendix, we address it in its own right.

I. Functional Specifications

The first document worked on in system development is the functional specifications.

II. Design Specifications

The next document worked on is the design specifications. As we said with respect to phased system development, the system construction phase can't be entered until functional and design specifications have been approved.

III. Program Documentation

During system construction, computer-program modules are developed. For each module, three documents are prepared.

A. Program Specifications

As we said with respect to controlling performance during program development, the first step in module development is writing the program specifications.

B. Program Structure Documentation

Also, as we said with respect to controlling performance during program development, program structure is documented before coding begins.

C. Annotated Code

A third document produced during module development is the program listing. Program listings are produced as a by-product of compilation. The question is, Are program listings documents? That is, are they readable? The answer is, They are if the programmer comments his code appropriately as he writes it. You should expect this from the programmer as a matter of course. Also, his job description should call for him to comment his code according to installation standards. And these standards should require the following.

1. Use of meaningful data names. You can enforce this use by conventionalizing the data descriptions used.
2. Organization of the code as specified in the program structure document.
3. A descriptive note before each routine or other functionally identifiable block of code.

If such standards don't exist in your installation, establish and enforce them for your project.

The programmer should recognize his self-interest in developing *annotated code.* The purpose of annotated code is to make the code readable when it comes time to modify it. One such time is when the programmer finds an error during unit testing. By making the code readable, the programmer makes his unit testing more efficient.

IV. System Integrity Test

Besides program module documentation, several other documents are produced during construction. One of these is the *system integrity test.* This test consists of a test plan, test data, and predetermined results for the system.

The system integrity test is prepared for use when the system goes into production. A production system is subject to change. A danger with such change is that, when a change is made, it may not only alter the system as desired, it may also alter the system in unanticipated and undesired ways. The system integrity test is used to detect such undesirable alterations. After a modification is made and tested, the modified system is run against the system integrity test to make sure it performs as desired before putting it into production.

Development of a system integrity test is a project responsibility and should be a requirement for the maintenance group to accept the system as maintainable. If you anticipate the need to develop a system integrity test, the economical way to develop it is as a subset of the link test.

V. Operations Manual

Another document produced during construction is the operations manual. As we said with respect to testing in controlling performance during construction, the last step in link testing is to have the computer center simulate production by use of the operations manual.

VI. User Manual

Yet another document produced during construction is the user manual. As we said with respect to testing in controlling performance during construction, the user manual must be prepared before user training can take place. And as we pointed out with respect to acceptance testing, part of this test is the use of the system by user personnel. They can't use the system until they've been trained.

VII. Conclusions

We've now discussed the following documents:

1. Functional specifications.
2. Design specifications.
3. Program specifications.
4. Program structure documentation.
5. Program listing.
6. System integrity test.
7. Operations manual.
8. User manual.

If you have these documents, you have a well documented system. Every one of these documents is developed as a by-product of system development. Thus, if you run your project as you should, there should be no great effort toward the end of the project to develop system documentation.

VIII. Documentation Maintenance

Documentation not only means developing documents. It also means keeping them up-to-date.

When documents are developed, they're then distributed. When a document is revised, the already distributed documents must be revised, and the recipients of previous distributions must be encouraged to update themselves by reading the revisions; so make it easy for the recipient to both revise his copy and update himself. Thus, the recipient must never be required to write anything to revise his documents. Either the whole document is reissued, or if the revision is less whole-sale, revised replacement pages are issued. This second approach requires that the document be issued in looseleaf.

Also, there must be, in a revision document, an indication of what was revised, so the recipient can read only the revised information. This is done by use of a *revision bar*, a narrow vertical line in the left margin to indicate content changes and additions. Corrections of clerical errors needn't be marked. Moreover, the document and each revision must carry a date so a record can be kept of what the latest version of a document is.

Finally, when a document is issued, a list of recipients must be established and maintained, so when a revision is made, it can be distributed to all current document holders. The best place for this list is in the document.

INDEX

Absence, 103, 107
Acceptance test, 45, 53, 54, 90, 126
Activity, 57, 58, 66, 84, 85
Actual time, 74, 77, 78, 81, 101
Algorithm, 85–88, 90, 186
Analyst, 93
Annotated code, 198, 199
Application knowledge, 88, 89
Arrow diagram, 65
Attrition, 102, 106

Backend loading, 98–100
Bar chart, 94–100, 102, 103
Bargaining, 80
Benchmark, 53, 54
Bubble, 65
Bubble chart, 66, 68, 69, 71, 94, 95, 97, 100, 175, 176
Budget, 38, 47, 74, 112–114, 161
Built-in turnover, 106, 107

Calculation, 87, 88
Calendar day, 77, 78, 97
Channeling communications, 139, 140
Checkpoint, 83, 91, 120–124, 141, 151, 195–197
Clear performance goals, 148, 151, 158
Code, 86, 97
Communication, 2, 91, 135–137, 140, 158
Company meetings, 103, 107
Comparative other, 148
Computer center, 50, 125, 127, 130, 135, 145, 146
Computer time, 56
Computer time cost, 111, 112

Consistency, 82, 83
Construction, 49, 55, 56, 90, 91, 107, 124–127
Contingency, 102–107, 114, 123, 141, 156, 158
Contingency allowance, 57, 75, 90, 102, 103, 105, 114
Contingency checklist, 104
Contingency level, 103, 104, 114
Conventions, 130
Coordination, 1, 117, 135–137, 139, 140, 156, 158
Copy library, 130
Cost benefit analysis, 48, 91
Cost estimate, 37, 50, 55, 89, 91, 108–112, 114, 116, 117, 193, 194
Cost responsibility, 49, 51, 52
Critical path, 93, 98
Critical path time, 98
Critical task, 92

Data rearrangement, 87, 88
Deadline, 38, 52, 73, 74, 94, 95, 98–101, 105, 106, 113, 114, 118–120, 141, 145
Decentralization, 40
Decision making, 87, 88
Deliverable end product, 83, 84, 120, 121
Delivery commitment, 105, 106, 133
Delivery date, 73, 74, 90, 94, 95, 98, 99, 102, 104, 106
Design, 49, 55, 56, 91, 93, 124–127, 129, 130
Design alternatives, 131
Design review, 51
Design review committee, 50, 90, 130
Design specifications, 49, 50, 52, 53, 90, 129, 198, 199
Designer, 93